THE RHYTHM BOOK

INTERMEDIATE NOTATION AND SIGHT-READING

By Rory Stuart

PLAYBACK+
Speed • Pitch • Balance • Loop

To access audio visit:
www.halleonard.com/mylibrary

Enter Code
2779-8726-8562-9246

Design and layout by Matthew Heister

ISBN 978-1-5400-1258-6

Visit Hal Leonard Online at
www.halleonard.com

Contact Us:
Hal Leonard
7777 West Bluemound Road
Milwaukee, WI 53213
Email: info@halleonard.com

In Europe contact:
Hal Leonard Europe Limited
Distribution Centre, Newmarket Road
Bury St Edmunds, Suffolk, IP33 3YB
Email: info@halleonardeurope.com

In Australia contact:
Hal Leonard Australia Pty. Ltd.
4 Lentara Court
Cheltenham, Victoria, 3192 Australia
Email: info@halleonard.com.au

"We were fortunate to get into a world of complex rhythmic possibilities for several days without speaking the same language and in the end left wanting more. Rory shows the rhythm with a captivating way with passion and boundless."

- CARLOS "CHARLIE" RUEDA
(Music educator, Aula Moderna de Musica y Sonido, Bucaramanga, Colombia)

"Professor Rory Stuart has been an inspiration for generations of jazz musicians for decades. His rhythmic approach is innovative and engaging, and his playing and composition skills are second to none. This is a fundamental book for every jazz musician."

- DR. RICARDO PINHEIRO
(Professor at Universidade Lusíada de Lisboa, Portugal)

"Rory's rhythm lessons opened a lot of doors for me. As a veteran player, I had spent many years focused on harmony; the lessons got me to concentrate on rhythm. Rory showed me ideas I was able to add and immediately utilize in my playing to make the music feel fresher. The lessons really influenced, and continue to influence, my playing."

- MICHAEL WOLFF
(Pianist, USA. Performed w/ Sonny Rollins, Nancy Wilson, Cal Tjader, Airto Moreira, Cannonball Adderley; coleader of Wolff & Clark Expedition)

"Some of today's musicians present their complex music in a way that causes anxiety and fear in both audiences and students. Rory Stuart presents his stuff with a smile, as if it were the most simple thing in the world, inviting others to follow."

- JAROMIR HONZAK
(Bassist, composer, and head of jazz program at the Academy of Performing Arts (HAMU), Prague, Czech Republic)

"As a fellow teacher who has studied rhythm with Rory, I can say he truly is a teacher's teacher. His precise and innovative instruction lifts my level of creativity and skill. His thorough coverage of rhythmic options allows for a massive expansion of concept, but he does it with an organizational structure in which it feels simple to learn and grow. Rory's method is genius and has taken so many young people to a new level that he has influenced a whole generation of jazz!"

- RACHEL Z
(Pianist, USA)

"Rory Stuart has a great ability to present advanced rhythmic concepts in a very organized and comprehensible way. At the same time, he is very aware of what music is really about: expression, emotions, spontaneity. His classes about rhythm not only expanded my knowledge of the theory of music, but also they helped me to use the new rhythmic devices in a thoughtful and tasteful way and to become a better artist."

- RAFAL SARNECKI
(Jazz guitarist and composer from Poland)

This book is for you if:

- You have completed *THE RHYTHM BOOK—Beginning Notation and Sight-Reading*, or you have a very solid command of rhythms on a basic level.

- You want to learn how to read and write more advanced rhythms.

- You already play an instrument (or sing) and read music, but want to refresh or strengthen your knowledge of rhythm notation, especially for more advanced rhythms.

- You compose or would like to compose music or write arrangements for others, and want to be able to correctly notate it.

- You are a music teacher who has worked through *THE RHYTHM BOOK—Beginning Notation and Sight-Reading* with your students and want a clear progressive method to teach the notation of more advanced rhythms.

- You are taking music classes, studying with a private instructor, or are teaching yourself.

Don't worry about your age, what instrument you play (including voice), or what style of music you play; understanding these more advanced rhythms and how their notation works will help you become a better musician.

This book has somewhat of an orientation towards jazz and contemporary music (funk, pop, rock, hip-hop, Afro-Cuban, Brazilian, modern classical) and includes the syncopation found in these styles of music and the swing feel of jazz. If you are an aspiring musician in a different style (e.g. folk, singer-songwriter), you can learn what you need to know about rhythm, but the book includes some "extra" rhythmic things not usually found in your style of music.

Rhythm is the key to so much in music. When you have read this book and completed the exercises in it, you will understand rhythmic notation, and be able to read and write any rhythm.

Please note: once you have completed this book, you will be ready for the other books in *THE RHYTHM BOOK* series. A natural next book for you is *THE RHYTHM BOOK—Rhythmic Development and Performance in 4/4*.

Table of Contents

Preface

You are looking at one in a collection of books that have taken many years for me to complete. They build upon my experience at the world renowned New School for Jazz and Contemporary Music in New York where, since 1992, I have designed and taught the rhythm curriculum. I've also been musical director or teacher at jazz workshops and clinics in Europe, Asia, South America, and the USA, and have had the opportunity to teach many remarkably talented students who have gone on to do impressive things musically. My experiences with the wide variety of students who have come to my classes and workshops with different musical backgrounds, different aptitudes, and different learning styles, have informed these books. Rhythm is of critical importance to the music but woefully under-represented in instruction materials and music education programs around the world. I hope these books will help address this need.

As I described in more detail in the preface to THE RHYTHM BOOK—Beginning Notation and Sight-Reading, the master drummer Keith Copeland, who played in my quartet through the 1980s, and Martin Mueller, the Director of the New School for Jazz and Contemporary Music, played instrumental roles in leading me on the path to teaching rhythm, and I am grateful to them.

Thanks are also due to the people who have helped specifically with this volume: Dan Greenblatt for specific, very thoughtful feedback on some pedagogic issues, as well as tips about publication of musical instruction books; Bob Sadin for insightful comments and especially for help on the Articulations section; Cody Rowlands (legato for brass); John Riley for several helpful suggestions; Christian Salfellner for his suggestion about triplet 16ths; Collin Bay and Andrew Bart for helpful feedback related to publishing; and Alfie Hole, for comments on the entire volume and Finale help as my research assistant beginning in late 2015; Natalie John, whose voice you hear on the recording of some exercises, and Noah Becker, who was a great help with MIDI files; the entire team at Hal Leonard, including Keith Mardak (Chairman & CEO, first to express interest in publishing the books), Jeff Schroedl (Executive Vice President who supported me through each stage of the process), and Debbie Seeger (Production Editor); the New School for Jazz and Contemporary Music for help with funding a research assistant, and Pam Sabrin for help in applying for this funding.

Special thanks are due to that research assistant, Matt Heister. Matt has been of so much help, in many ways, with the nitty-gritty. He not only did layout/design, but also brought great ideas and feedback about musical content and presentation on so many levels—he has the perfect combination of patience, attention to detail, and expertise in just the right combination of areas, and without him, I don't know how I would have gotten this book completed! When he completed his time as a student, he graciously continued to work with me on the books.

A generous Fulbright Scholar Award for four months in 2013-2014, with the support of New School, helped me get more time to work on the book, during my first sabbatical in 21 years. Thank you to everyone at Fulbright who helped (special thanks to Hana Rambouskova), and to my host school Janácek Academy of Music and Performing Arts (special thanks to Vilem Spilka).

A small circle of people who are important in my life provide love and support that make everything (not just these books) possible—thanks always to Tuck & Patti, Chris, Liz, Carole & Avery, Bob, and, Marc!

Finally, as one who learned so much on the bandstand, I want to acknowledge that my many musical colleagues throughout the years contributed indirectly to this book (too many to name here, but please see my acknowledgments of them on the my website: www.rorystuart.com), as have my hundreds of students through the years (for a small sample of them, see the "teaching" page on my website. A large number of people in the jazz world, who organize workshops and clinics, and run clubs, festivals, performance spaces, and schools, are highly intelligent and capable people who could easily receive more money or fame doing other things but do what they do out of love for the music, and make so many things possible; thanks to all of you! Fellow teachers and musicians around the world have also helped, especially in making me aware of the need for this book—some have gone out of their way to keep in touch and ask "when will the books be finished and published?!" Thanks!

How to Use This Book

There are three elements to this book: 1) the text and written examples and exercises; 2) the worksheets; and 3) the recorded examples.

As you read through the text, you will see written exercises for you to sight-read. Recordings of some of these are provided so that you can check that you are reading them correctly. Please note the distinction between **Examples** and **Exercises** (they are numbered differently); I recommend you study both, but also practice the exercises.

A separate stack of worksheets is included on Hal Leonard's My Library website so that you can practice writing rhythms. Some of them are used to practice correcting notation, some are for you to create your own examples, but many are for you to transcribe recorded examples.

Recordings of the exercises feature different sounds: voice, percussion, or piano. In some cases, there is more than one recording of an exercise.

You can sight-read each exercise, then use the recording to check yourself. You can practice transcribing rhythms using the worksheets. If you feel you need more transcription practice and less sight-reading, you can listen to and transcribe some of the recorded exercises before you look at them in the book, then use the book to check your work.

To access the recordings of exercises from the text, transcription examples for the worksheets, and selected examples, go to: www.halleonard.com/mylibrary.

Note: if you want to speed up or slow down any of the recorded exercises, use the *Playback*+ program included with Hal Leonard's My Library.

The author would be delighted to hear from you, so, please write if you have questions, comments, or suggestions. To contact the author, as well as see updates, corrections, additional examples, a forum, and blog supporting the books, please visit www.RoryRhythmBooks.com.

> Occasionally, there are observations that may be of interest to the teacher of rhythm or to the student who wants to get into greater depth, but are not essential for the general reader. These sections are shown with a gray shaded box like you see here.

Introduction

This book is for those who have already mastered quarter-note, eighth-note, and triplet-eighth-note rhythms (as taught in *THE RHYTHM BOOK—Beginning Notation and Sight-Reading*).

You may at first find some of the material covered in this book (including 16th-note and triplet-16th-note rhythms, odd meters, and triple meters) intimidating. However, the rhythms with which you are already comfortable provide a solid foundation on which you can systematically build mastery of this more advanced material.

I recommend using this book at your own pace, being certain to understand each step before you move on to the next. To move at a faster pace through any sections you find easy, skip some of the exercises. If you find the material in any section to be difficult, make up additional exercises of your own for that section.

The additional exercises you create may be completely new inventions using the material we are covering, or they may be supplemental exercises to help you do an exercise in the book which you initially find to be difficult (we might call this "breaking down a rhythm").

In order to "break down a rhythm," here are some specific approaches you can take in creating your own supplemental exercises. Imagine that the exercise you come to is this one (Exercise 2-067 on page 29, but without its pickup):

You can create an exercise that repeats just the end of the phrase in the correct place in time.

Exercise 2-001:

With this and all such supplemental exercises, repeat each plenty of times so that you are confident and relaxed doing it before going on to the next one. Next, add some more to the beginning:

Exercise 2-002:

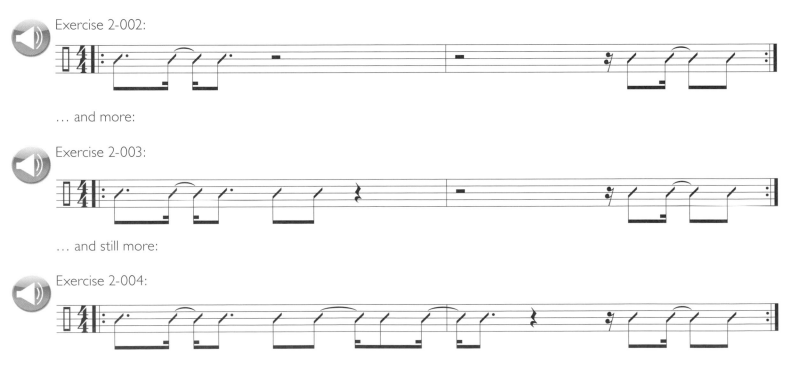

… and more:

Exercise 2-003:

… and still more:

Exercise 2-004:

… until you are ready to go back and sing the entire phrase.

There are other ways the same exercise could be broken down into a progression of supporting exercises. For example, start with just the end:

Exercise 2-005:

… and add:

Exercise 2-006:

… continuing until you get to this:

Exercise 2-007:

… and so forth.

Or, you could even break the phrase down starting at a target point in the middle of it, like this:

Exercise 2-008:

… and building it like this:

Exercise 2-009:

… then:

Exercise 2-010:

… then:

Exercise 2-011:

… and finally, playing the entire original exercise, including the last two beats.

Though you would not need to do this for an exercise that is immediately easy for you, this process of "breaking down" and then building back up one step at a time can be very helpful when you come upon an exercise that you initially find to be difficult.

Rhythms in 4/4

In *THE RHYTHM BOOK—Beginning Notation and Sight-Reading*, we looked at notation and sightreading in 4/4 at the levels of quarter note, eighth note, and simple triplet eighth. If you have worked through that material, or are already familiar with it, you are ready to examine rhythms at the 16th-note level and beyond, including triplets, in 4/4.

16th-Note Rhythms

We will start with 16th-note rhythms. This builds directly on the knowledge of eighth note notation.

Introduction to 16th-Note Rhythms

As we saw in *THE RHYTHM BOOK—Beginning Notation and Sight-Reading*, eighth notes divide the quarter-note pulse into two equal parts. As discussed in that volume, it is important that we show required beats (which, in the case of 16th-note rhythms, is every quarter note); and don't show unrequired beats. Now we turn to 16th notes, which divide the quarter note pulse into four equal parts. Musically, we find 16th-note rhythms in a variety of styles of music and different musical situations; for example, in funk music, double-time lines in a swing context, or Brazilian music written in 2/4.

A **16th note** looks like this: (♪) if it is by itself. As you can see, it looks similar to an eighth note, but it has two flags rather than one; its two flags always point "forward" (to the right). A 16th note can also be beamed to other 16th notes, like this:

Like all notes, these can be shown in standard notation, indicating pitches instead of the rhythmic notation we've been using. In standard notation, here are the same 16th notes:

A **16th note rest** looks similar to an eighth note rest but with a second "hook:" ♬

Beaming 16th Notes and Rests

With 16th notes, a simple rule is to beam together all the notes that are a part of one beat. So, we would not leave the notes from one beat as orphans:

Example 2-001:

... but rather, beam them:

Example 2-002:

Even if there is a rest in the middle of the notes that make up one beat, we will include them in the beam, although we have a choice of two slight variations, a standard beam:

Example 2-003:

… or a beam with "half stems" to the rests.

Example 2-004:

The one place where a couple of completely different beaming styles may be used is if the rest is at the beginning or the end of the beat. In this case we can choose to "beam rests" (this is what I personally advise), i.e. put a beam across all the notes and rests that make up each quarter note; but not everyone prefers this style of beaming.

In this example, we see figures with rests at the beginning and end of their beats, in the style where the rests are beamed (notice that, in the first beat, we show a rest of an eighth note, rather than two 16ths, in keeping with our rule to not unnecessarily show unrequired beats):

Example 2-005:

… and in the style where these rests are not beamed:

Example 2-006:

The reason I personally usually prefer beaming the rests is that it makes it easier for one's eye to immediately discern what belongs to each beat (and makes it clear, for example, that the figures are not triplet 16th notes). Notice that, in an example such as this one, it can take a bit of work for the eye to discern the "boundaries" i.e., where it is that one beat ends and the next begins:

Example 2-007:

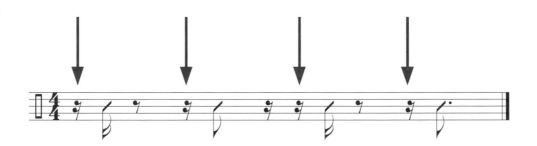

However, I will include some examples in which the rests are not beamed, as you need to be accustomed to reading either notation.

Worth noting is that, in order to consistently follow our rule ("for music at the 16th level, beam by beat"), you may have to beam eighth notes differently in a measure that has 16th notes than in one that does not. So, in the following example, because it is on the eighth note level (i.e. the finest division of time in the measure is an eighth note), we would only show beats "one" and "three." Thus, we would beam the last two beats this way:

Example 2-008:

… yet in this example, with 16th-note rhythms earlier in the bar, the last two beats, which would sound the same, would be written this way:

Example 2-009:

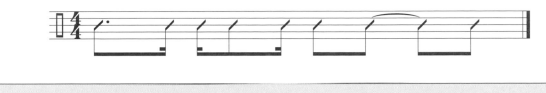

> There are a variety of stylistic choices for notation that are acceptable and easy to read, and other choices that should be avoided. For example, through most of this book I have not half-stemmed beamed rests, yet doing so is a completely acceptable (and, by some, preferred) alternative. Please see Appendix VI for further discussion of this and other stylistic choices and rules for notation.

Correct Poorly Beamed 16th Notes

In order to be sure you are confident about how to correctly beam 16th notes, it is useful to practice correcting poorly beamed examples. For instance, here is an example where there is no beaming at all:

Example 2-010:

To correct it, we simply draw beams beat by beat to connect all the notes that are part of a beat:

Example 2-011:

In the next example, there are beams mistakenly drawn to connect one beat to another:

Example 2-012:

Correct it by removing any beam that crosses from one beat to another:

Example 2-013:

Here's an example that beams notes in a somewhat arbitrary way, sometimes failing to beam together notes that are part of the same beat, and also sometimes beaming notes between beats:

Example 2-014:

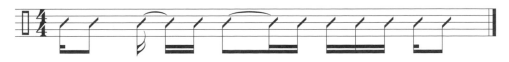

Correct that by mentally grouping each of the notes that are part of a particular beat, and then beaming them accordingly:

Example 2-015:

Practice correcting poorly beamed examples using Worksheet 2-W-001.

From Eighth Note to 16th Note

Let's build on the rhythmic vocabulary you already have—particularly quarter note and eighth note rhythms—as the foundation to your mastery of 16th-note rhythms.

In *THE RHYTHM BOOK—Beginning Notation and Sight-Reading*, we saw the exact correspondence between quarter-note-level figures in 4/4 and eighth note-level figures in 2/4. This allowed us to create well-notated bars of eighth-note rhythms in 4/4 by simply combining the 2/4 rhythms. There is a similar correspondence between these quarter-note figures in 4/4, eighth-note figures in 2/4, and 16th-note figures in 1/4. A well-notated bar of 4/4 at the 16th note-level looks like four well-notated beats of 16th figures, so, as a first step, let's look at each of the possible 16th-note figures. As we discussed, the 16th figures should be beamed by beat; although we have a choice of whether or not to beam rests. Note that we are looking at each place a note or notes could fall on the 16th note grid, but then notating so it is easiest to read. Thus, in the first example, a single note falling on the first 16th of the beat we simply show as a quarter note (which could have a staccato mark if we want it to sound for a short duration).

Let's look at each of these corresponding figures at the quarter-note, eighth-note, and 16th-note levels:

Example 2-016:

Example 2-017:

Example 2-018:

Example 2-019:

Example 2-020:

Example 2-021:

Example 2-022:

Example 2-023:

Example 2-024:

Example 2-025:

Example 2-026:

Example 2-027:

Example 2-028:

Example 2-029:

Example 2-030:

Possibilities for 16th-Note Figures per Beat

We can consider every variation, not just of when the note is played, but how long it is sustained. Here are all of the possible figures that can happen. Repeat signs are used to enclose figures in which the notes are played at identical places, regardless of how they are sustained. I've organized them into the possible 1-note, 2-note, 3-note, and 4-note figures. Practice singing each of these:

Example 2-031:

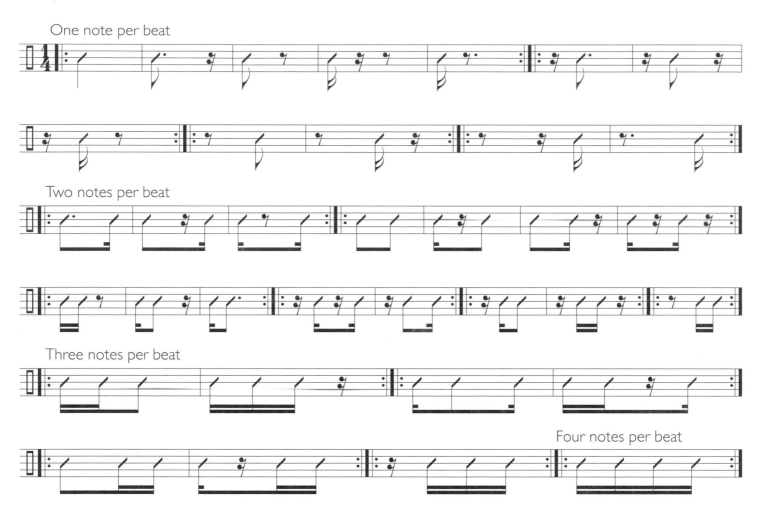

Notice that in a couple of bars, I've shown the exact same figure, but writing it with or without dotting the eighth note rest.

In the above example, the rests are separated; here are the figures shown with the rests beamed:

Example 2-032:

Two notes per beat

In the interest of showing every variation that can be written, I've included some that would rarely be written except where it is necessary to be extremely precise about note duration. If we remove these, our list of figures looks like this:

Example 2-033:

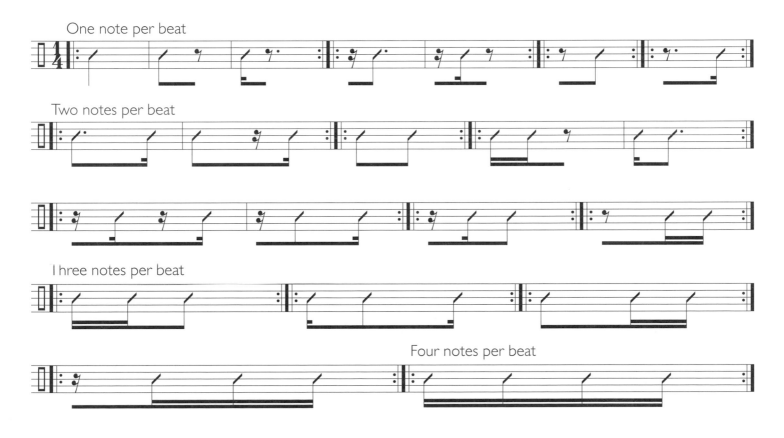

Try singing through the figures in Example 2-033 as an exercise.

Combining 16th-Note Figures in 4/4

Now that you have seen all of the possible figures, here are some exercises that let you practice reading them when they are combined to make bars of 4/4. If you notice any figure or combination of figures that you find at all difficult, isolate those figures and create exercises for yourself so you can concentrate on just those figures.

> As described in depth in *THE RHYTHM BOOK—Beginning Notation and Sight-Reading*, there are many ways of practicing the rhythmic exercises, and these can help you to physically internalize the rhythms. These include different combinations of singing, clapping or tapping or finger-snapping, and walking or foot-tapping (see Appendix II). For example, walk quarter notes and clap your hands on beats "two" and "four" while you sing the written rhythm. Just as that book described the possibility of practicing eighth note exercises singing the "name" of where each note falls by 'name' (the name from calling the eighth notes "one and two and three and four " - so one might sing "one and two … four and"), a similar option is to do the same with 16th-note rhythms (calling the notes "one ee and ah, two ee and ah, etc.," sometimes abbreviated "1 e + a"). I do not ask students to do this, but some other teachers do. I suggest you try this and see whether you feel it helps you or not.

At first, we will practice reading different combinations of the 1-note per beat figures:

Exercise 2-012:

… then combinations of the 2-note per beat figures:

Exercise 2-013:

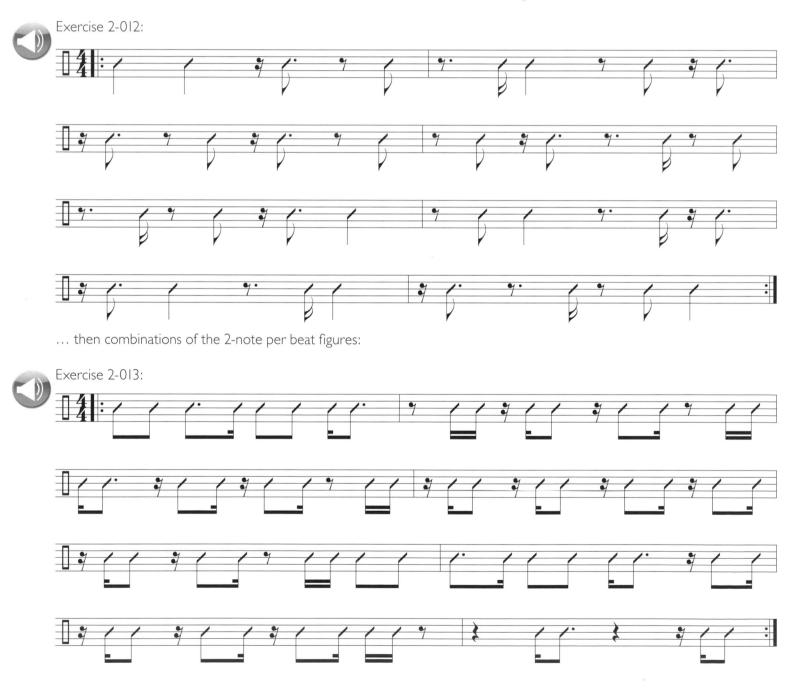

… and combinations of the 3-note per beat figures:

Exercise 2-014:

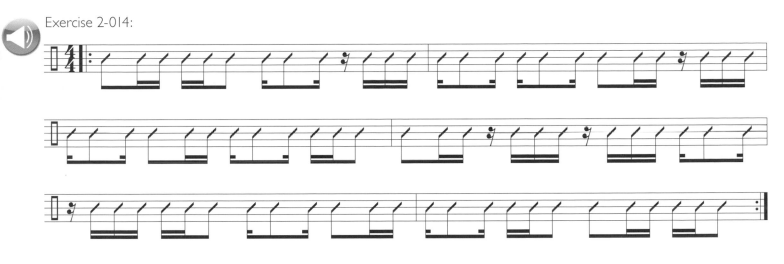

Did you notice that the more notes per beat there are, the easier it is for you to read the rhythm? I've found this is commonly true for most of my students.

Now that we've systematically worked on 16th-note figures with different numbers of notes per beat, let's combine them in the following short series of exercises.

This exercise combines 1- and 2-note per beat figures:

Exercise 2-015:

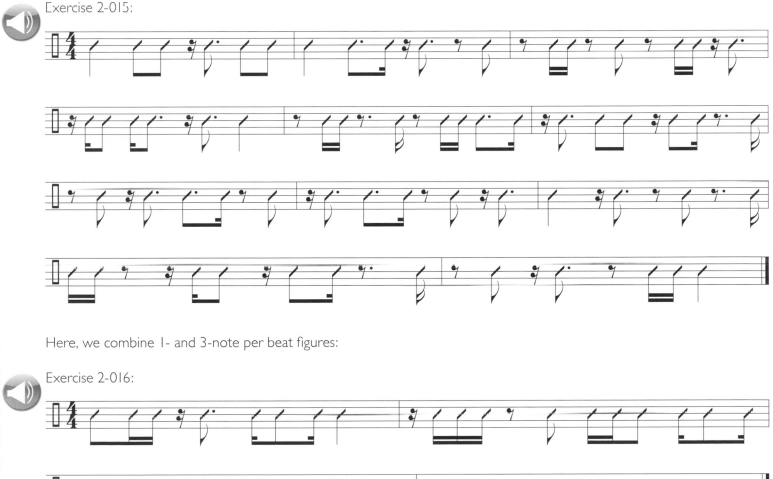

Here, we combine 1- and 3-note per beat figures:

Exercise 2-016:

Here are combinations of 2- and 3-note per beat figures:

Exercise 2-017:

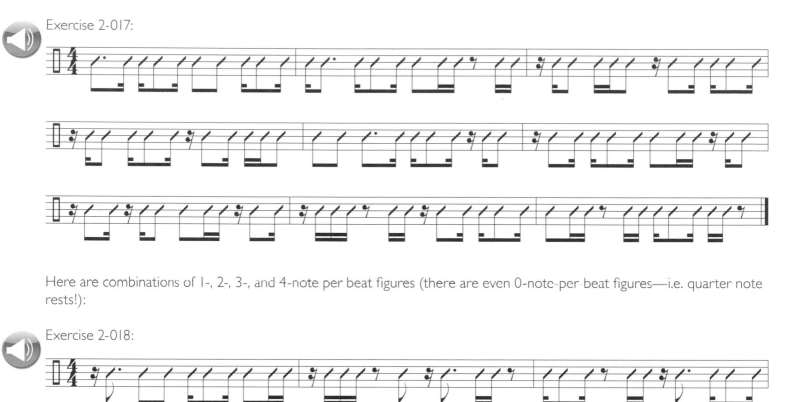

Here are combinations of 1-, 2-, 3-, and 4-note per beat figures (there are even 0-note-per-beat figures—i.e. quarter note rests!):

Exercise 2-018:

Of course, once we allow ourselves to combine any of the 0, 1, 2, 3, and 4-note per beat 16th-note figures as we did in this last exercise, we can write everything possible that can happen at the 16th-note level!

Why Do Many People Have More Difficulty with 16ths Than Eighths?

We will look at and practice many more exercises, but it is worth first considering the issue of "difficulty." Given that there is the exact correspondence between the quarter-note figures that can happen per measure of 4/4, the eighth-note figures that can happen per half note, and the 16th-note figures that can happen per beat, shouldn't all of these be equally easy to read and write? In fact, since the way each beat is beamed is so clear at the 16th-note level, perhaps 16th-note rhythms should be less difficult than eighth-note rhythms, in which your eyes have to work to see the separation of the bar into two halves.

Yet, many of my students at first find that 16th-note rhythms are not as easy to read and write. For some, 16th-note rhythms are initially much more difficult and, for others, at least somewhat more difficult. If this is not the case for you, a discussion of this may merely satisfy your curiosity about why this is an issue for others; but, if you are finding 16th notes more difficult to read, it may be useful to think about the reason(s) for this.

Initially, 16th-note rhythms may seem difficult because you think "they are so fast." But it is not necessarily the case that they are fast—depending on the tempo set in the count off, 16th notes in one example may be slower than eighth notes in another.

This 16th note example at its metronome marking:

Example 2-034:

... is slower than this eighth note example:

Example 2-035:

> A word about metronome markings: they show a note value and a number that represents beats per minute. Thus, a quarter note followed by an equal sign and then by the number 60 means there are 60 quarter notes per minute (one per second); a quarter note followed by equal sign and the number 90 means there are 90 quarter notes per minute; and so forth.

Another reason may be that it feels more difficult to divide a beat into more parts: 4 equal parts for 16th notes versus 2 equal parts for eighth notes. If this is the case for you, you will quickly find that it just takes some practice to become accustomed to this.

Another reason, perhaps less obvious, that is likely the most common one at the heart of this difficulty is that of familiarity. The jazz or contemporary musician is constantly exposed to music at the eighth-note level. Turn the pages of any typical "fake book" (book of the melodies/chord changes to tunes, i.e. "lead sheets"), and you will likely see page after page of eighth note music with only the occasional 16th notes.

This would not be true if it were a book of Brazilian tunes as notated by Brazilians (who typically write sambas, for example, in 2/4 at 16th-note level). But fake books will often show even these Brazilian tunes as eighth note music in cut time (we will discuss "cut time" below).   So, an example that a Brazilian composer would notate like this:

Example 2-036:

... will instead be written like this (the symbol ₵ represents 2/2, i.e. measures look just like 4/4, but are felt as two beats each, with those beats written as half notes):

Example 2-037:

You would also see a lot of 16th notes if it were a book of transcriptions of funk charts by a group such as Tower of Power. But, whether old Tin Pan Alley tunes (standard American show tunes from the first half of the 20th century), bebop tunes, or many modern tunes, we find many eighth note examples and far fewer 16th-note examples. If you are less familiar with the 16th-note figures, don't be surprised if, at first, you find them more difficult.

To solve this problem, expose yourself to more 16th note music, especially syncopated 16th note styles. If you aren't finding fake books that help with this, a great solution is to create your own examples.

Create Your Own 16th-Note Examples

Two approaches you might choose in creating your own 16th-note examples are 1) constructing them to address difficulty you have reading and writing certain specific figures; or 2) using eighth note music as source material.

Practice Specific Figures

To address problems with specific figures, imagine that you find yourself having difficulties with these two:

Exercise 2-019:

Create an exercise such as this one and practice it until it is easy for you:

Exercise 2-020:

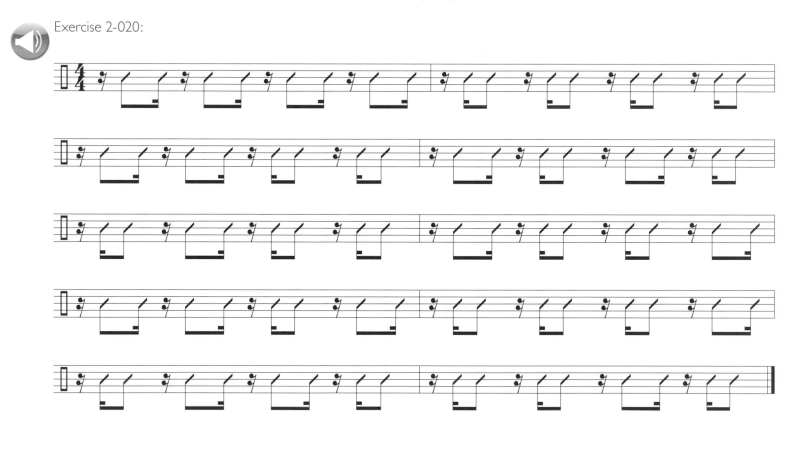

If you have problems with these three figures:

Exercise 2-021:

... you might write an exercise such as this one:

Exercise 2-022:

So whatever figures you find to be tricky, or even if there are some that you find require a bit more effort or concentration, write an exercise with focus on them, using them over and over and combining them in different ways.

Incidentally, although I'm suggesting you include the rests when you beam by beat, you will sometimes encounter music where this has not been done, so be sure you are also able to read things if they are written this way:

Exercise 2-023:

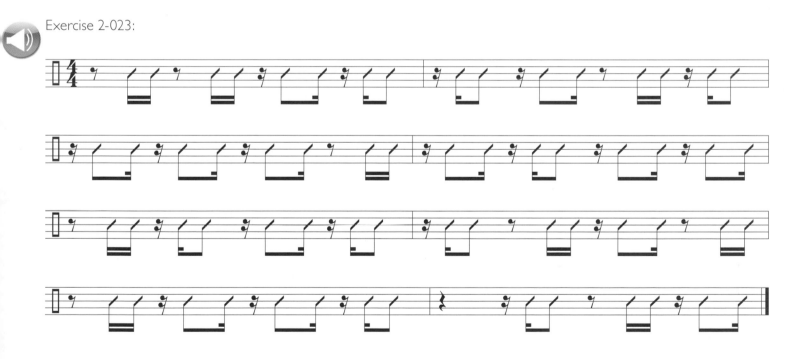

Create your own exercise, with focus on any figures you find tricky, using Worksheet 2-W-002.

Then practice transcribing 3 notes per beat figures using Worksheet 2-W-003; 2 notes per beat figures using Worksheet 2-W-004; 1 note per beat figures using Worksheet 2-W-005; and examples that combine all of these using Worksheet 2-W-006.

Convert Eighth Note Examples to 16ths

The second approach, in order to generate more 16th-note examples, is to take syncopated eighth note music as source material and convert it to 16th-note exercises that are written twice as fast.

For example, take the kinds of rhythms found in a bebop song (the eighth notes should be swung):

Exercise 2-024:

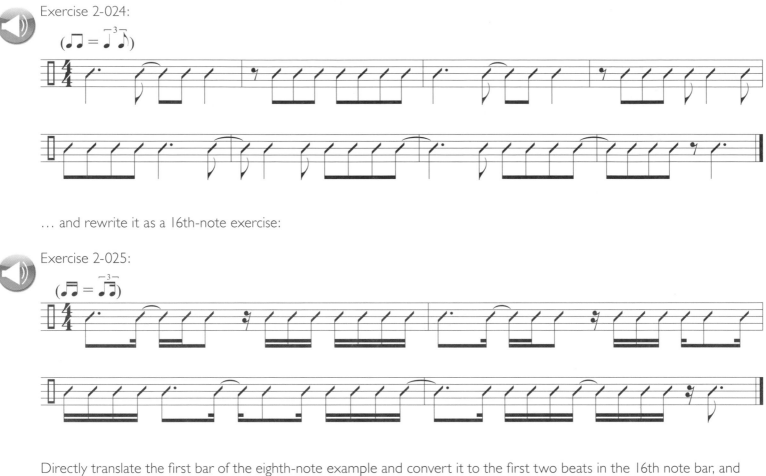

… and rewrite it as a 16th-note exercise:

Exercise 2-025:

Directly translate the first bar of the eighth-note example and convert it to the first two beats in the 16th note bar, and the second bar of eighth notes to the last two beats in the 16th note bar.

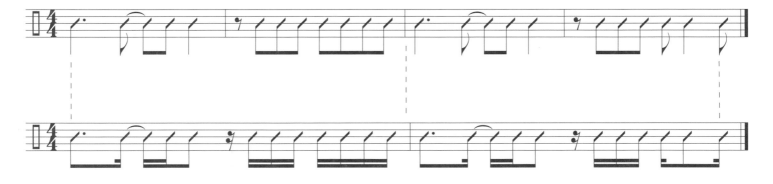

Notice that you can sing the rhythms exactly as you did in the eighth note version—if your count off is half as fast, there is no need for the melody to be any faster than it was in the eighth note example, and you can swing the 16th notes in Exercise 2-025 as you swung the eighths in Exercise 2-024.

The process of rewriting is quite straightforward: take the rhythms from each two beats of eighth note rhythm (first two beats in the bar, then the second two beats) and convert them to rhythms that are twice as fast and last for a quarter note (first beat in the bar, then second beat in the bar, etc.). The transformations of each figure are exactly those we saw in Example 2-016 through Example 2-030. Of course, the second half of the bar of 16th notes will come from the second bar of eighth notes.

Here is another instance of syncopated eighth notes:

Exercise 2-026:

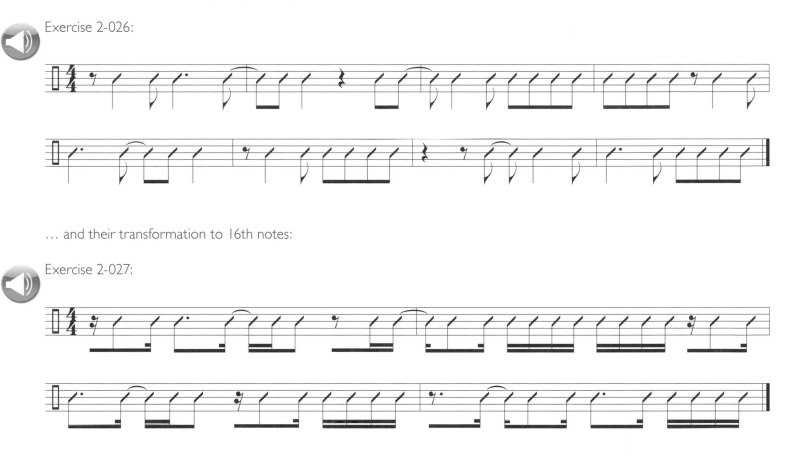

... and their transformation to 16th notes:

Exercise 2-027:

Practice converting eighth-note rhythms to 16th-note rhythms, using Worksheet 2-W-007.

Count Offs for 16th-Note Examples

In *THE RHYTHM BOOK—Beginning Notation and Sight-Reading*, we already suggested some tips for doing good count offs. A count off for 16th-note music can be the same as one for eighth note music. The only additional suggestion for counting off music at the 16th-note level is to make certain you are feeling the 16th-note "grid" very clearly and strongly (singing it in your mind) before you do the count off.

Tied 16ths

As was the case with eighth note level rhythms, tied 16th notes can prove challenging if you are not accustomed to reading them—you may find that it helps to internally "mark" each beat, even as you sustain notes over the beat—practice with this fairly long exercise:

Exercise 2-028:

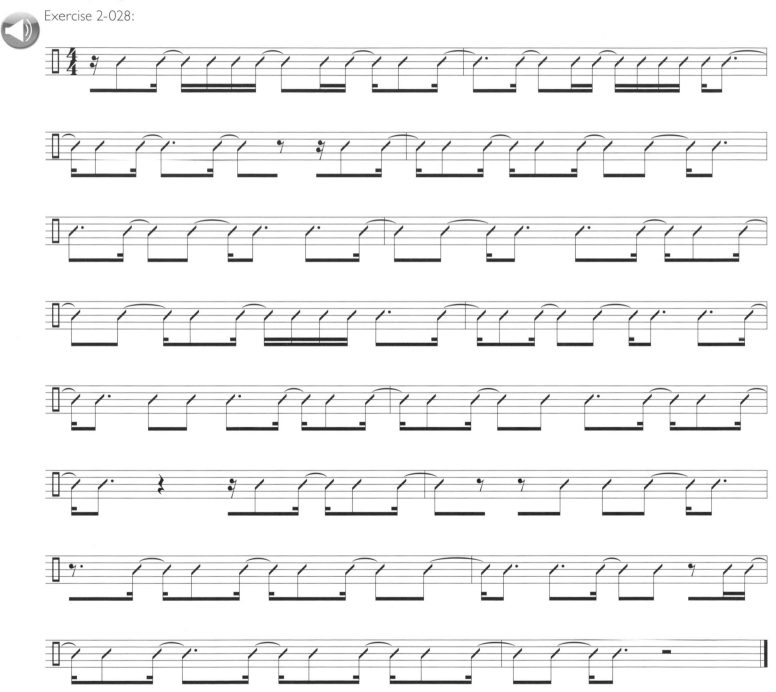

If you need more practice reading ties and are short on material, create your own, either from scratch or by adding ties to an existing piece of music. For example, here's a 16th-note exercise:

Exercise 2-029:

and here is what you might do to convert Exercise 2-029 into an exercise to practice reading ties:

Exercise 2-030:

In Worksheet 2-W-008, create your own exercises by choosing some places to tie figures from one beat to another.

Short and Long Notes

Notice that, at the 16th-note level, notes can be written long or short (i.e. they can be sustained or not). Here is a version in which notes are long:

Example 2-038:

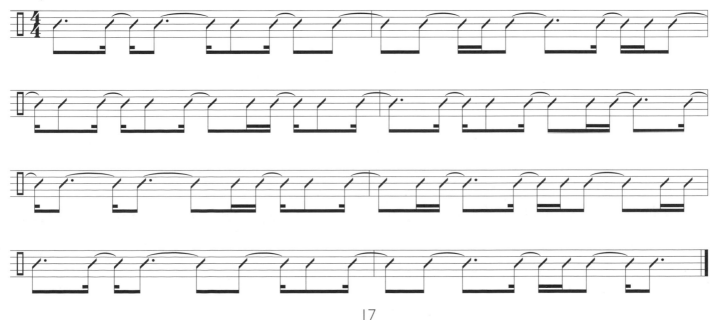

And here are the same rhythms written short:

Example 2-039:

Incidentally, also look at this example if written without beaming the rests on either end of each beat:

Example 2-040:

 In Worksheet 2-W-009, convert between long and short versions of the rhythms.

Pickup 16th Notes

As with the eighth-note exercises we practiced in *THE RHYTHM BOOK—Beginning Notation and Sight-Reading,* 16th note music can have pickups and it is worthwhile to practice reading and transcribing exercises that incorporate pickups. Note that, while the rule is that we do not precede the first note in a pickup bar with any rests, some people fill in the beginning of the individual beat on which the pickup begins with rests in a pickup bar. As long as there are "missing beats" in the bar before the first written music, it will be clear that this bar is a pickup.

Read these short exercises that include pickups:

Exercise 2-031:

Exercise 2-032:

Exercise 2-033:

Exercise 2-034:

Exercise 2-035:

Exercise 2-036:

Exercise 2-037:

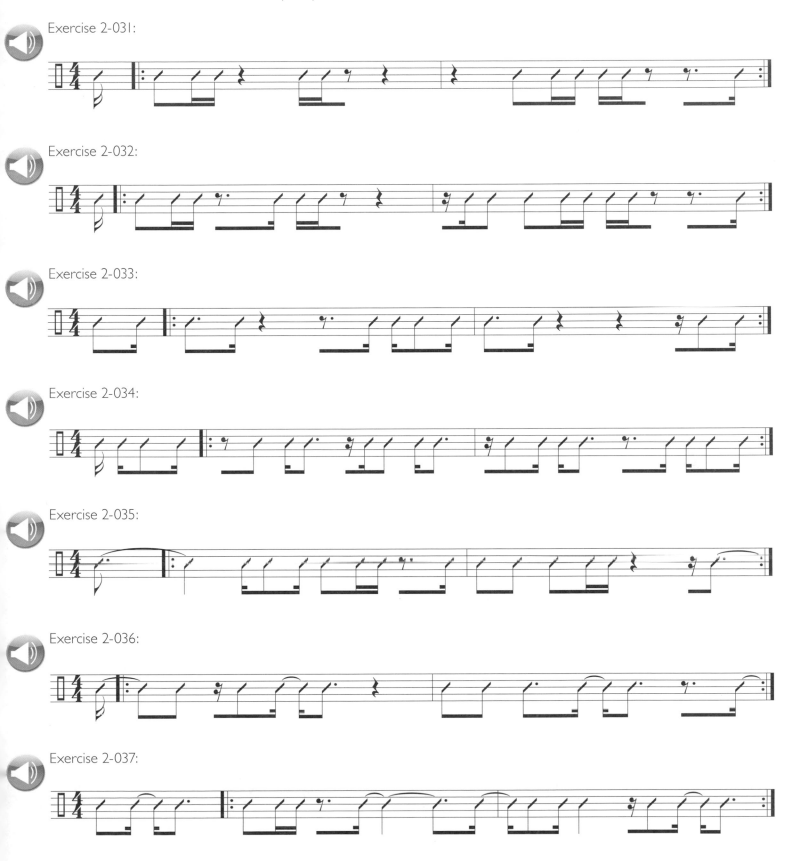

Feeling Each Part of the Beat

It is important to really be able to feel each part of the beat at the 16th level, in a precise way. Consider the difference between this:

Example 2-041:

… and this:

Example 2-042:

… or the difference between this:

Example 2-043:

… and this:

Example 2-044:

You will not last long in a funk band if one is called for and you mistakenly do the other! In fact, for a wide range of styles that use 16th-note rhythms, it is important to play these kinds of distinctions very clearly.

Sing these exercises to practice making clear the distinctions between different parts of the beat:

Exercise 2-038:

Exercise 2-039:

Exercise 2-040:

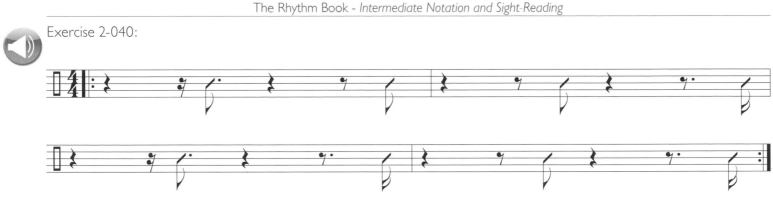

 Practice transcribing some exercises like this using Worksheet 2-W-010.

Note Density Revisited

As often proves to be the case, fewer notes can make reading rhythm more difficult. The following tests your ability to keep track of the underlying beat; focus on feeling each quarter note, either internally or with the help of tapping your foot, as you accurately sing this exercise:

Exercise 2-041:

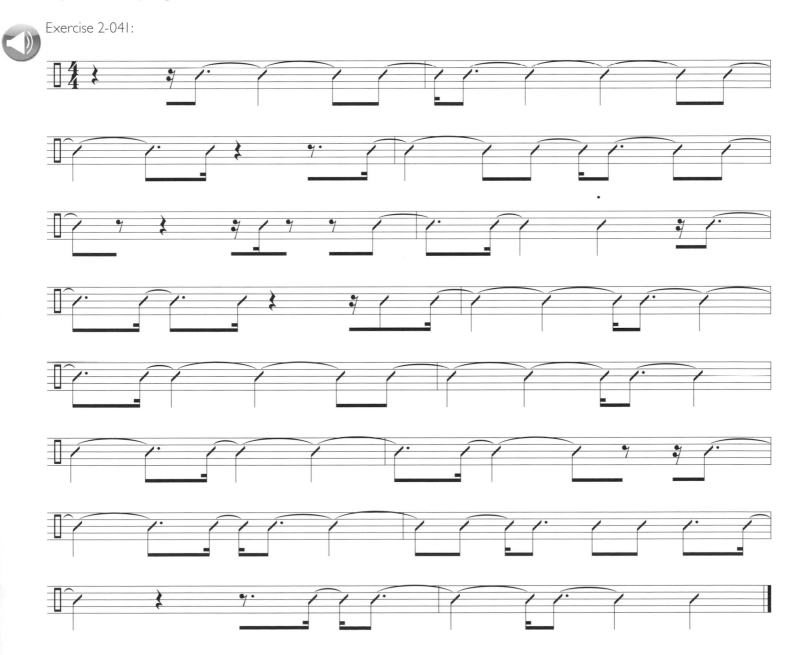

If the previous exercise proves difficult for you, one helpful exercise you can do takes the start of one figure at a time and displaces it to different beats so you get comfortable with it (In this example, I'm addressing the figure in Exercise 2-041 that starts in the first bar, and the figure that starts on the end of the third bar):

Exercise 2-042:

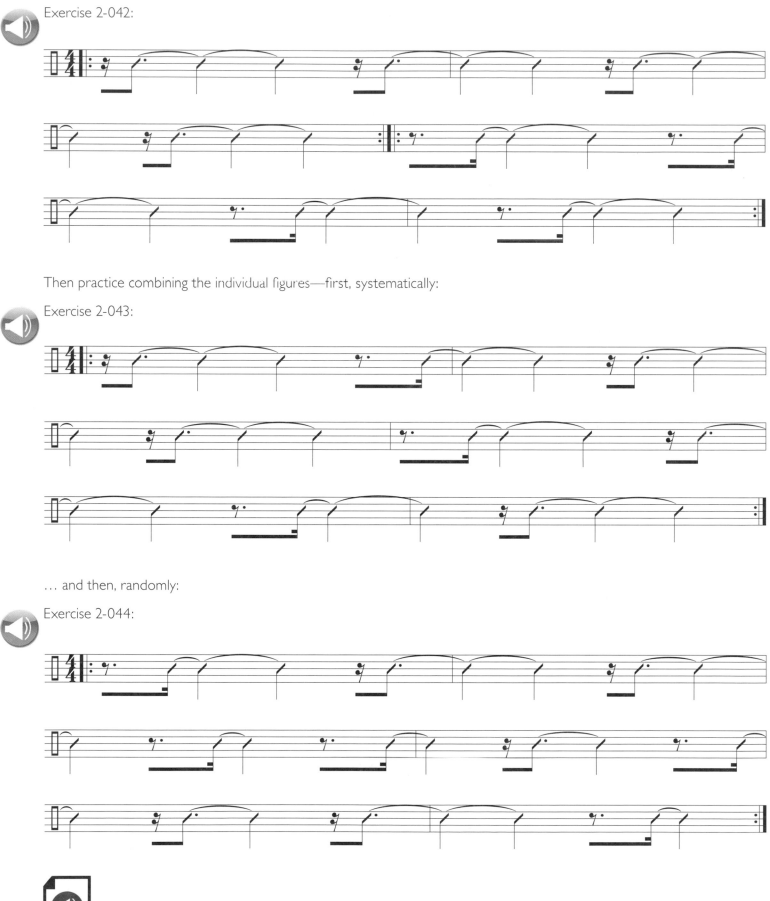

Then practice combining the individual figures—first, systematically:

Exercise 2-043:

... and then, randomly:

Exercise 2-044:

Practice transcribing some sparse examples with Worksheet 2-W-011.

16th Notes Can Swing!

You may be familiar with swinging eighth notes but assume that 16th notes are always played with a straight feel. This is not necessarily true. To take two obvious examples, if you notate a Charlie Parker (or other bebop) solo and the soloist plays double time feel lines, they are almost always played as swing 16th notes. So in a passage such as this, the 16th note lines are likely played with swing feel:

Example 2-045:

You can indicate this in text if you want the person reading it to be certain:

Example 2-046:

swing 16th notes!

Similarly, many funk and hip-hop grooves are at the 16th-note level but have a bit of shuffle to them. Try reading this exercise with straight 16th feel, and then again but with swung 16ths:

Exercise 2-045:

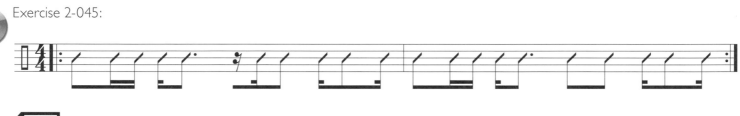

Transcribe examples, some using swing 16ths and some using straight 16ths, with Worksheet 2-W-012.

Correcting Poorly Notated 16ths

In a classic "crazy things that can happen on the road" experience I had, I played with a great jazz organist who had charts that did not follow the notation principles we have discussed—and they were difficult to read! (For more about that experience, see Appendix 1). The music itself was terrific, but not difficult—it was the way in which it was written that made it tricky. If one looked at a bar of his written music the first time, it was difficult to decipher, for a number of reasons.

Here is the kind of thing he would write – this is not from an actual chart of his, but the kind of wacky notation he would use:

Example 2-047:

Before we speak about the rhythmic elements, notice what he did with accidentals: he (arbitrarily) mixes sharps and flats, and the flats in the key signature are used—but there are no courtesy accidentals. By the last part of the measure, one's head is spinning trying to keep track of which notes are sharp, natural, and flat; then, in the next measure, he starts again with a new, different (and arbitrary!) series of mixed sharps and flats!

With courtesy accidentals, it would look like this:

Example 2-048:

… but, with more consistent use of accidentals that make sense with the key signature, it would look like this:

Example 2-049:

But now, we get to our focus, the rhythmic notation. Notice these two properties of his style of writing: 1) because you can never see the required beats, if you play anything wrong in the beginning of a measure, there is no way to see where you are and "recover" during that measure—so, any mistake in the beginning ripples through, causing everything else to be played incorrectly; 2) every measure is filled with a large number of unfamiliar rhythmic figures that you have likely never seen before and will never see again.

Most of the actual music in these charts was grooving and rather simple syncopated rhythms—once you hear it, it makes sense, it only seems so difficult because of how it is written. I'm sure some people would address the problems posed by these charts by hearing each piece and memorizing how the rhythms (and the music) actually sound. This could work but notice two problems with it: 1) there is a lot to memorize (more than 200 charts, as I remember); and 2) the first time through you must listen rather than play. So, this is a problematic strategy—in a band like this, if you get the gig and don't play the written music the first time through each chart, you could be fired before you ever get a chance to memorize things!

A better strategy is to help yourself read things better—there likely would not be time to actually rewrite the charts, but lightly pencilling in a well-notated version of the rhythms can be a huge help.

In order to correct the notation, we first need to be able to see what happens on each beat. With experience, you will do this in your head, and be able to immediately write the corrected version. At first, however, it may help to have an intermediate stage. Since the music is at 16th-note level, we can first write out every 16th note, beamed by beat:

Example 2-050:

Next, we want to see where each note falls:

Example 2-051:

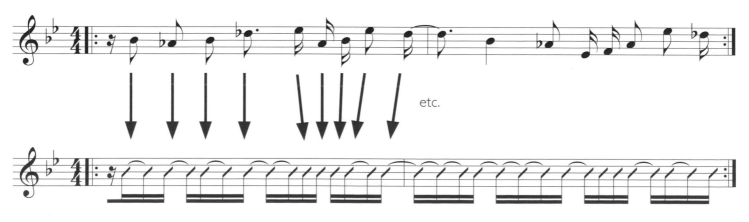

We can now see what happens on each beat—but, though we see the required beats, we have introduced another problem: we are unnecessarily showing unrequired beats (we do not need to show every 16th note!). We do not want to have any ties between notes that are part of the same beat, so we simplify, while keeping each beat separate. If you pencil in well-notated rhythmic notation such as this above each bar, it will be a great help in accurately playing the music!

Example 2-052:

Of course, if you were writing the chart yourself rather than pencilling in helpful corrections, you would use pitches, and it would look like this:

Example 2-053:

Let's try correcting another example that fails to show required beats, looking at only the rhythms. Here is the poorly-notated version:

Example 2-054:

Here is the intermediate stage, in which you account for every 16th note:

Example 2-055:

... and here is the final corrected version, in which only required beats are shown:

Example 2-056:

Here is one more poorly notated example:

Example 2-057:

... with an intermediate stage that shows what happens on each beat:

Example 2-058:

... and a final corrected version that eliminates unrequired beats:

Example 2-059:

Not only will skill in correcting poorly notated examples serve you well should you ever get into a situation with charts like those by the great jazz organist with whom I played; your practice in this process will help you avoid making these kinds of mistakes in your own writing.

 Practice correcting poorly notated examples in which required beats are not shown, on Worksheet 2-W-013. Practice correcting notation in which unrequired beats are shown unnecessarily, using Worksheet 2-W-014. Practice correcting examples that have a combination of different mistakes in notation with Worksheet 2-W-015.

16th Note Practice in 4/4

We will look at some more exercises to practice reading 16th notes in 4/4.

Here are four short exercises without ties or pickups:
Exercise 2-046:

Exercise 2-047:

Exercise 2-048:

Exercise 2-049:

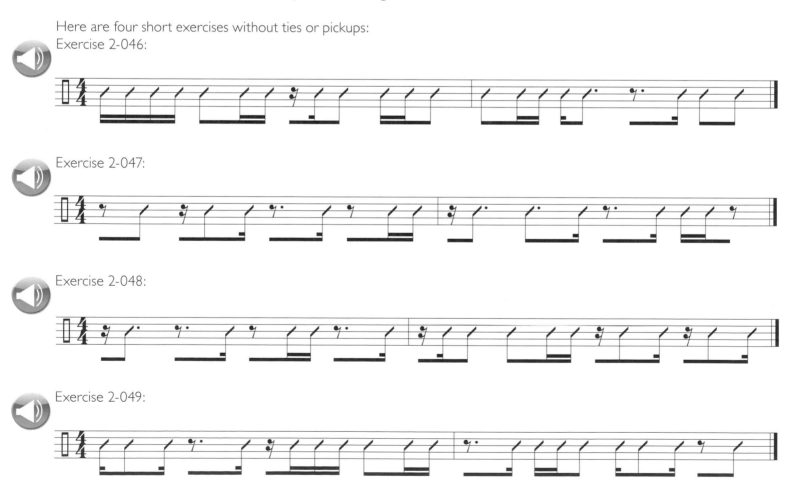

These exercises include pickups:

Exercise 2-050:

Exercise 2-051:

Exercise 2-052:

Exercise 2-053:

Exercise 2-054:

Exercise 2-055:

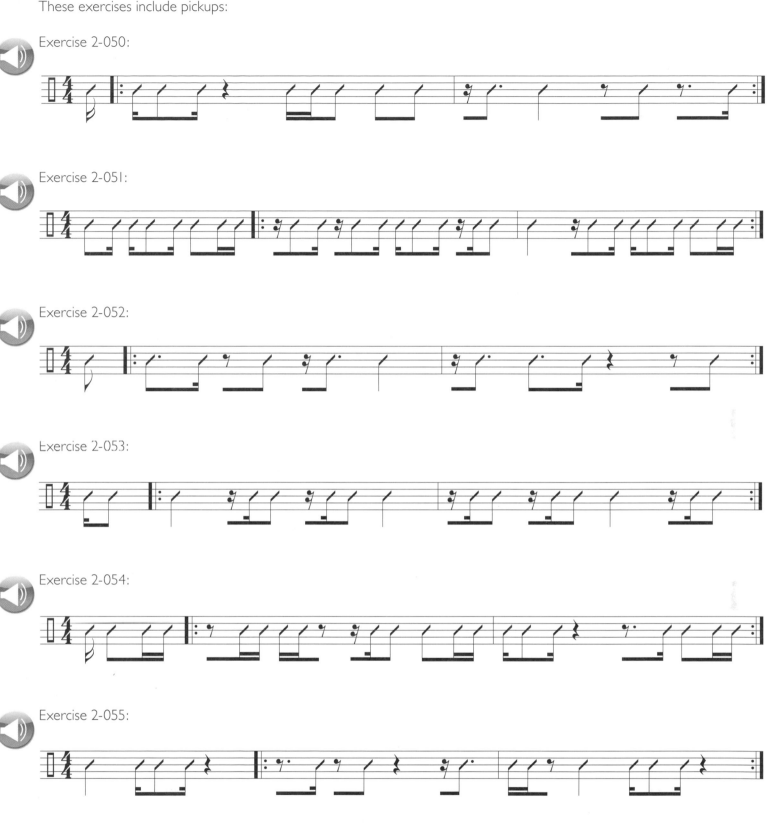

Here are some exercises that will help you practice reading 16th-note rhythms with ties:

Exercise 2-056:

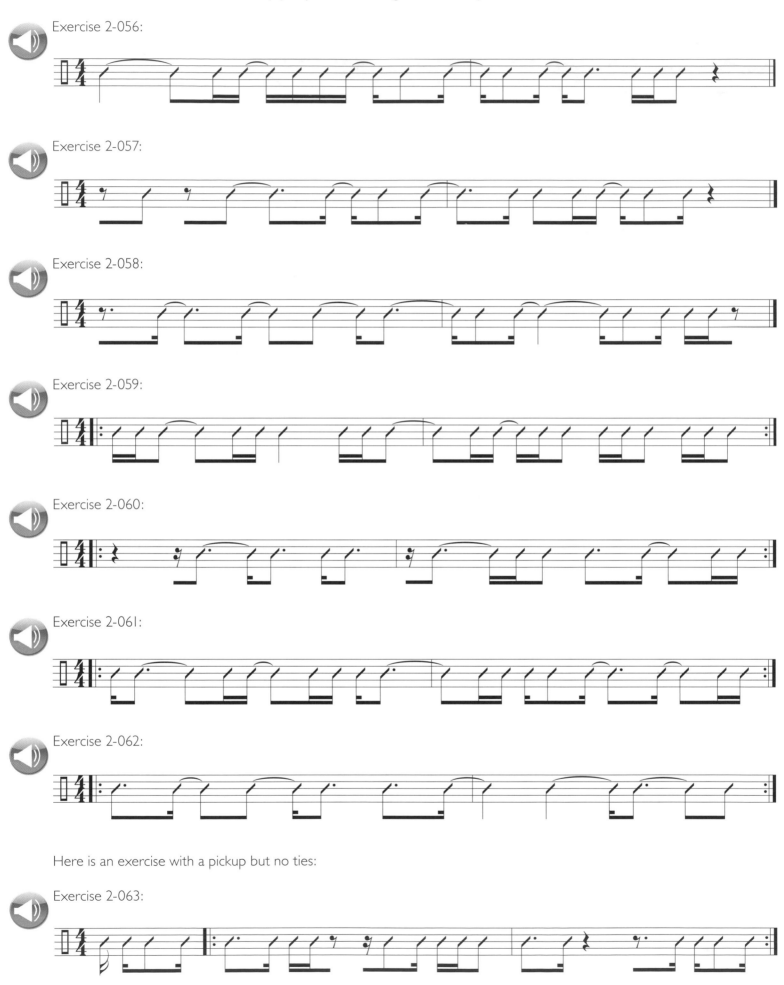

Exercise 2-057:

Exercise 2-058:

Exercise 2-059:

Exercise 2-060:

Exercise 2-061:

Exercise 2-062:

Here is an exercise with a pickup but no ties:

Exercise 2-063:

The following exercises include pickups and ties. Notice that Exercise 2-064 is identical to the previous exercise, but with ties added:

Exercise 2-064:

Exercise 2-065:

Exercise 2-066:

Exercise 2-067:

The next three exercises are similar to each other—an idea with different variations.

Exercise 2-068:

Exercise 2-069:

Exercise 2-070:

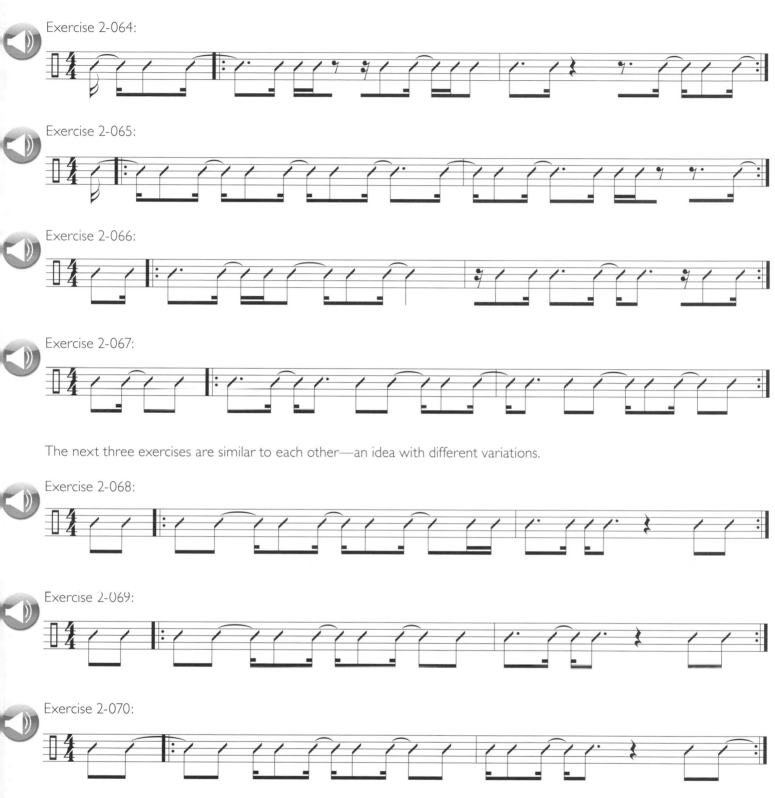

By this point, I am giving you some truly tricky 16th note syncopated rhythms to sing. Do them as slowly as you need to, feeling grounded in where each beat is, and confident that you are singing the rhythms of each beat correctly.

Exercise 2-071:

16th-Note Exercises with Pitch

Now, we will look at some 16th-note exercises written in standard notation with pitches. As we discussed in *THE RHYTHM BOOK—Beginning Notation and Sight-Reading* when we introduced pitches with eighth notes, if necessary, ignore the pitches the first time you read any that you find difficult, then sing the pitches the second time. If you can already read them both simultaneously, that is great—but, at first, give priority to reading the rhythms correctly.

First we start with a short exercise written in rhythmic notation:

Exercise 2-072:

… then with pitches:

Exercise 2-073:

Here is another exercise to practice reading 16th-note figures:

Exercise 2-074:

And here is the same 16th-note exercise with pitches (and a bar added at the end). Notice that, in this and other exercises, we write half rests rather than two consecutive quarter rests at the beginning or end of measures. Although we want to show each beat at the 16th level, there is no need to write consecutive rests at the beginning or end of the bar:

Exercise 2-075:

Here is an exercise you have read before (Exercise 2-028) but with pitches:

Exercise 2-076:

Here is one more exercise with pitches at the 16th level:

Exercise 2-077:

Multi-part 16th-Note Exercises

Finally, we practice reading some multi-part 16th-note exercises, both with and without pitches.

Read this version without pitches:

Exercise 2-078:

… and then this rhythmically identical version but with pitches:

Exercise 2-079:

Another exercise without pitches:

Exercise 2-080:

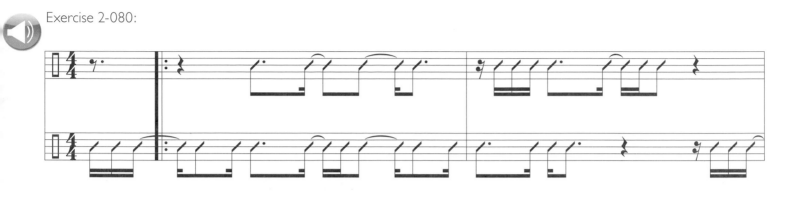

... and a version with pitches:

Exercise 2-081:

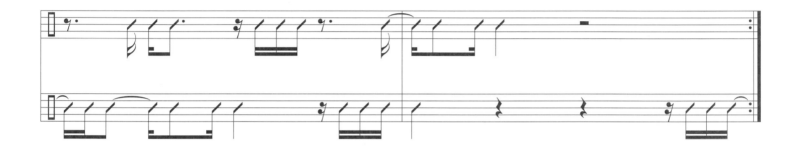

Notice that, in this exercise, unlike some of the multi-part exercises we have looked at so far in this book and in *THE RHYTHM BOOK—Beginning Notation and Sight-Reading*, the challenge is not to always play a rhythmically independent part, but to play your part with the other parts, sometimes separating briefly to become rhythmically independent. A version without pitches:

Exercise 2-082:

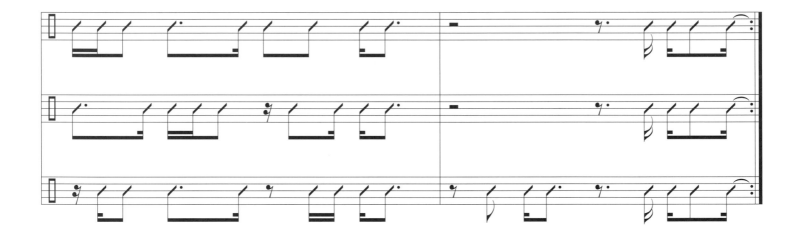

… and the same, but with pitches:

Exercise 2-083:

 Practice transcribing multi-part 16th-note examples on Worksheets 2-W-016, 2-W-017, and 2-W-018.

Triplet Half Notes, Triplet Quarter Notes, and Broken Triplet Eighths

In *THE RHYTHM BOOK—Beginning Notation and Sight-Reading*, we introduced eighth note triplets and observed that notes within the triplet can be tied. Here is a quick review:

Review of Eighth-Note Triplets: The Meaning of the Triplet Sign

First, let's make sure we understand the meaning of the triplet sign. If you are only familiar with eighth note triplets, you might think something such as "the triplet sign means the notes under it are squeezed to fit into one beat." But that does not truly capture what the triplet sign means—as we see when we look at other rates of triplets. For example, these triplet quarter notes take the time of two beats, not one:

Example 2-060:

So what does the triplet sign mean? The "3," by convention, means "3:2" (three in the time of two). When we see a triplet sign, it tells us to do a rhythmic superimposition in which we "squeeze" three into the time of two i.e. to play three notes so that they evenly divide the time that two would normally take. If there are three quarter notes worth of music, we squeeze them into the time normally taken by two quarter notes; if there are three half notes, squeeze them into the time normally taken by two half notes; if there are three 16th notes, squeeze them into the time that two 16th notes normally take; whatever is bracketed by the triplet sign, squeeze three to fit in the time of two.

In Example 2-060, there were literally three quarter notes bracketed by the triplet sign. But, as we saw with eighth-note triplets, there could be ties. If the first two notes were tied:

Example 2-061:

… the example would be better written by simplifying the first two tied quarter notes to one half note:

Example 2-062:

Now, when you look at this example written this way, you may at first think "there are not three notes, so how does the triplet sign work?" Upon consideration, you see that a half note plus a quarter note take a total of three beats, so the triplet sign would squeeze them into the time of two beats. So, the triplet sign is really telling us the rate at which the notes it brackets should be played.

> You may have found half notes and quarter notes to be easier than eighth notes, which are in turn easier than 16ths, which are easier than 32nds, etc. Interestingly, with triplets, many people initially find triplet eighths to be easier than triplet quarters, which are easier than triplet half notes. That need not be a cause for concern; a solid command of triplet eighths will serve as our foundation for mastering triplet quarter notes and triplet half notes, as you will see in the next sections.

From Triplet Eighths to Triplet Quarters

Let's use Carnatic (South Indian) syllables to help us accurately feel triplet quarter notes. First, we will sing triplet eighths, using the syllables "Ta-ki-ta:"

Exercise 2-084:

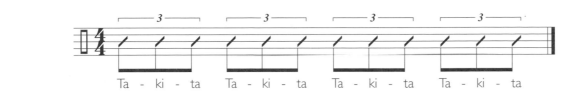

Next, sing the triplet eighth notes again but repeating the syllables "Ta-ka:"

Exercise 2-085:

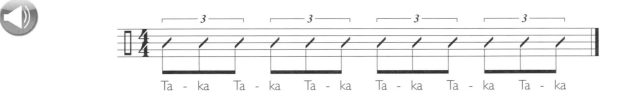

Next, feel the "Ta-ka's," but only sing the "Ta's:"

Exercise 2-086:

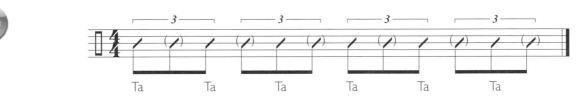

Just as a quarter note is twice as long as an eighth note, a triplet quarter is twice as long as a triplet eighth. Therefore, the attacks you are singing now are exactly triplet quarter notes. If you want to sing legato triplet quarter notes (sustaining each note for its full value), think the "Ta-ka's," but sing only the "Ta's," sustaining each until you sing the next one. Here is how it would look if you tie the triplet eighth notes:

Exercise 2-087:

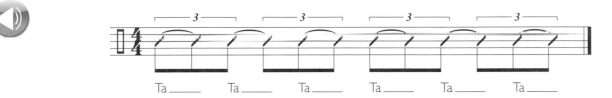

But, of course, two tied triplet eighth notes are the same as one triplet quarter note. So, if we simplify each beat individually, we get this:

Exercise 2-088:

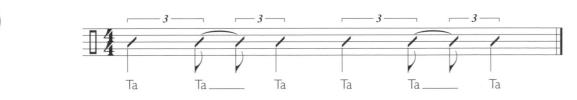

And that is identical to this:

Exercise 2-089:

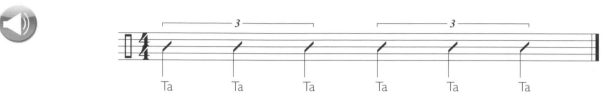

Ta   Ta   Ta   Ta   Ta   Ta

Here are the quarter-note triplet figures that can happen per half note:

Example 2-063:

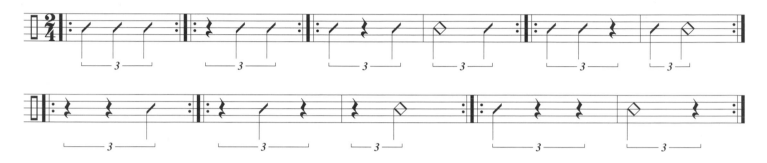

Notice that the figures within repeat signs sound identical except for note duration. Also, unless you are dealing with unusually slow music where note durations are exceptionally precise, there would be no reason to write the figures in the last two measures—one could write (with no triplet sign) a half note or quarter note instead.

From Triplet Eighths to Triplet Half Notes

While you may have been comfortable singing triplet quarter notes at any tempo even without the previous exercise, it is unusual for someone to be able to accurately sing triplet half notes at a very slow tempo unless they have a technique to relate these to a smaller subdivision—for example, to triplet eighth notes. Here is a technique for this.

First, sing triplet eighths, as you did before, using the syllables "Ta-ki-ta:"

Exercise 2-090:

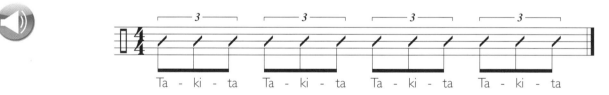

Ta - ki - ta   Ta - ki - ta   Ta - ki - ta   Ta - ki - ta

Next, continue singing the triplets, repeating the syllables "Ta-ka-di-mi." At first, say these syllables accenting the first note of each beat, so you feel totally locked into the tempo of the quarter notes:

Exercise 2-091:

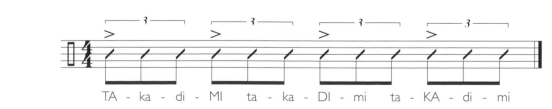

TA - ka - di - MI   ta - ka - DI - mi   ta - KA - di - mi

Continue, but now sing these syllables accenting the first "Ta:"

Exercise 2-092:

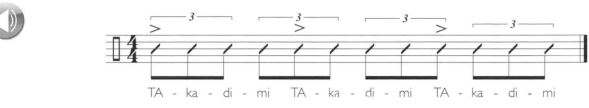

TA - ka - di - mi   TA - ka - di - mi   TA - ka - di - mi

Now, feel the "Ta-ka-di-mi" internally, but only sing out loud the first "Ta:"

Exercise 2-093:

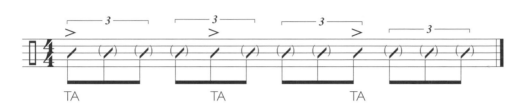

TA   TA   TA

Since a triplet half note is as long as four triplet eighth notes, our attacks are now exactly those of accurate triplet half notes. In order to sing legato triplet half notes, sustain each "Ta" until you sing the next one, internally feeling the entire "Ta-ka-di-mi" as you sustain the "Ta."

Here is how this looks with ties:

Exercise 2-094:

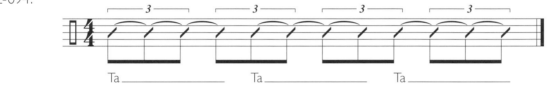

Ta_____   Ta_____   Ta_____

We can simplify it beat by beat:

Exercise 2-095:

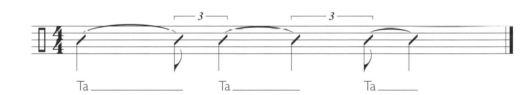

Ta_____   Ta_____   Ta_____

Or, alternately, simplify it to the triplet quarter level:

Exercise 2-096:

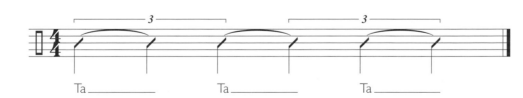

Ta_____   Ta_____   Ta_____

Then simplify it to the triplet half level (which we do just to prove to ourselves that what we have been singing is what we intended):

Exercise 2-097:

Ta   Ta   Ta

Incidentally, notice that Exercise 2-095 sounds identical to triplet half notes, but shows you how they feel beat by beat.

Principles of Notation at Triplet Levels

We have already discussed principles of notation for quarter notes, eighth notes, and 16th notes. Among these principles designed to simplify notation are: 1) show required beats; 2) beam by required beat; and 3) avoid showing unrequired beats when possible. So, in order to notate triplets well, we merely have to follow the same principles, knowing what the required beats are for triplets.

An easy rule of thumb is this: for any kind of triplet the required beats are those that would be required for the next faster level of duple note. The next faster level than a triplet half note is a regular quarter note; we know that at the quarter level in 4/4, we only have to show beat "one" and this is also true for triplet half notes. The next faster level than a triplet quarter note is a regular eighth note; we know that, at the eighth note level in 4/4, we need to show beats "one" and "three" and this is also true for triplet quarter notes. The next faster level than a triplet eighth note is a regular 16th note. We know that required beats to show for 16th note rhythms in 4/4 are "one" "two" "three" and "four" and this is true also for triplet eighth notes.

We do not need to be overly rigid with this rule in cases where your common sense says it is not helpful. For example, when the first two or more beats of a bar with triplets are silent, we can put in a half note rest, rather than put rests on every quarter. Similarly, a half note rest is fine if the second half of the measure is silent.

How to Write Quarter-Note Triplets That Begin on "Two" or "Four"

This leads us to an interesting problem: what if we want to notate something that sounds like triplet quarter notes that begin on beat "two" or beat "four?" Let's first consider the case of triplet quarter notes beginning on beat four. In the following example, we want the triplet quarters to begin on the last beat of the second bar, and continue (into the first bar) when the repeat happens.

Example 2-064:

But notice that what we've just written is obviously not correct! If you look at the second bar, it has too many beats, and the first bar has too few beats! If you were reading along from a previous measure and came to the first bar here, it would look quite confusing. When is the first note played (it looks like it is played right on beat "one")? Why are there too few beats in the first measure (a triplet quartet note is shorter than a regular quarter note, so there are fewer than four full beats) and too many notes in the second measure?

Similarly, if we try writing it in the following way, we have also got the wrong number of beats in each measure (we've just traded which one has too many beats and which has too few!)

Example 2-065:

The correct solution is to notice what happens on each beat (it is helpful to consider the relationship between quarter-note triplets and eighth-note triplets), and write it this way (notice that we also indicate "tacet 1st time" on beat "one" of the first bar so that music in that beat is only played the second time):

Example 2-066:

(tacet 1st ×)

This would be the best notation even if it were not within a repeat:

Example 2-067:

This is exactly what Peter Bernstein plays on "Solid Jack" from the Larry Goldings recording *Sweet Science*.

Example 2-068:

These notations that show beat "one" of each bar are unquestionably better. However, what about the case where a quarter note triplet begins on beat "two"? One possibility would be to write it like this:

Example 2-069:

However, we notice that notation hides beat "three." Recall that, with quarter-note triplets, the required beats to show are "one" and "three," as with regular eighth notes.

An alternative notation that shows the required beats is this:

Example 2-070:

Notice that this notation divides the middle triplet quarter note in half (as did the notation in Example 2-066 and Example 2-067), so that we can see beat "three."

My belief is that all principles of rhythmic notation that we follow should be working towards the cause of making the music as easy as possible to read. But Example 2-069 vs. Example 2-070 are an interesting case: I've asked a few hundred people over the past several years, and, while the response is divided, I think at least as many people prefer the notation in Example 2-069 to that in Example 2-070. So, "show beat three" at your discretion in this case; if you prefer not to, people will still probably do fine in reading what you have written.

It is possible also that the context of other things in the bar can change what people prefer to read. For example, some would find this:

Example 2-071:

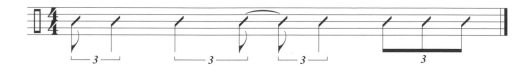

… preferable to this:

Example 2 072:

… even if they prefer Example 2-069 to Example 2-070. But even Example 2-072 is not bad. So, this seems like a rule that is good to understand (and always to apply for triplet quarter notes starting on beat "four"), but use your judgement whether to follow it for triplet quarter notes starting on beat "two."

One reason to consider choosing the Example 2-070 version is the confidence it inspires in those reading your music—they see you "know what you're doing," so can relax and trust that the other things you write will be cool.

Feeling Each Part of the Triplet
In getting more comfortable with triplet eighth notes, make sure you clearly feel each part of the beat. For example, practice this exercise:

Exercise 2-098:

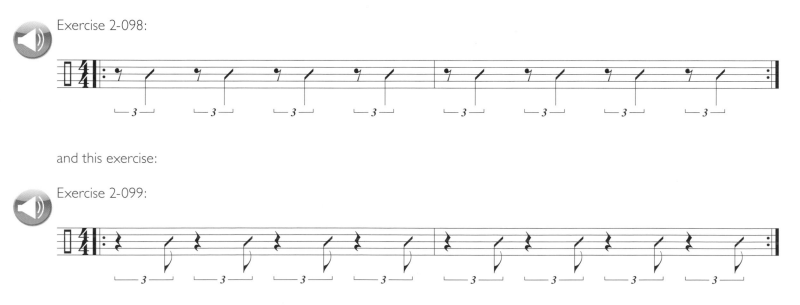

and this exercise:

Exercise 2-099:

You can also alternate, for example, this way:

Exercise 2-100:

Resist the tendency to make the "off-beats" you are singing become the new "on-beats;" feel where each real beat is and where what you are singing falls with respect to the beat.

"Broken" Triplets and Ties

At the eighth-note triplet level, consider what can happen within one beat. Here are the possible triplet-eighth-note figures per beat:

Example 2-073:

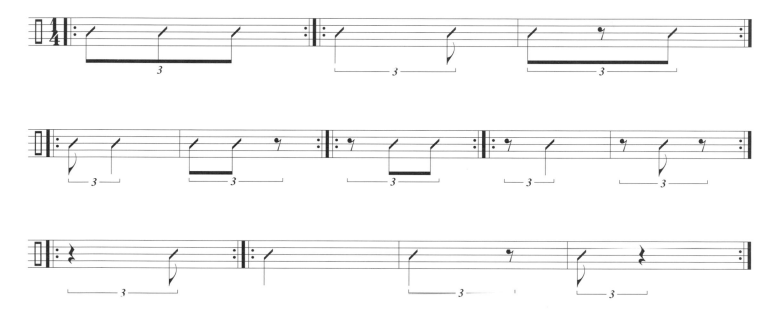

Notice there are a few more ways in which you could see a figure written, but I have not included them above because they are undesirable ways to write them. All of the following figures unnecessarily show unrequired beats (you do not have to show every triplet eighth note at this level, just every "beat," and there is better notation that sounds the same in Example 2-073):

Example 2-074:

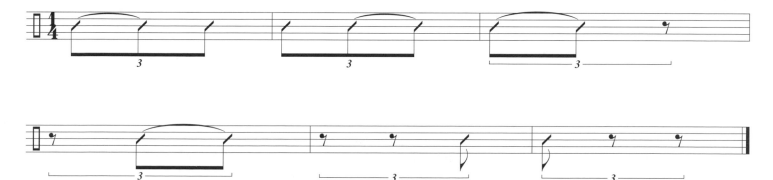

Combine the well-written triplet figures per beat in different ways and practice reading them:

Exercise 2-101:

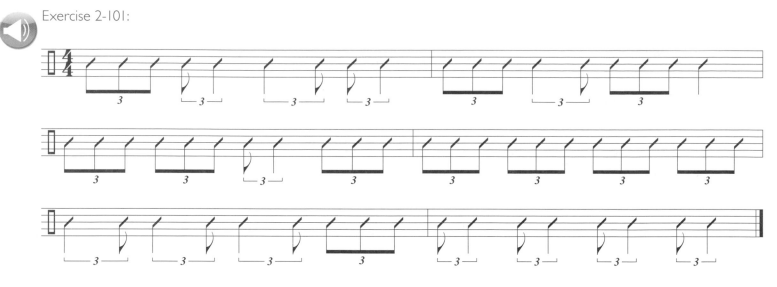

Notice that using pitches can convey some rhythmic shapes not apparent from purely rhythmic notation. The following is identical to the previous example, but with pitches:

Exercise 2-102:

Here are the same figures but with some notes tied:

Exercise 2-103:

Practice these exercises that combine triplet-eighth-note figures:

Exercise 2-104:

Exercise 2-105:

Exercise 2-106:

Try reading the following example, which is rhythmically the same as Exercise 2-106, but with pitches:

Exercise 2-107:

Practice transcribing triplet-based examples using Worksheet 2-W-019.

Triplet Eighth Groupings

Triplet eighth notes can be grouped in different ways, some of which cause their pattern to shift in time. As discussed in *THE RHYTHM BOOK—Crossrhythms on 4/4*, a repeating pattern that does not evenly divide the measure and keeps shifting in time is called a "crossrhythm."

Triplet eighth notes grouped in twos:

Exercise 2-108:

Triplet eighth notes grouped in fours:

Exercise 2-109:

Triplet eighth notes grouped in fives:

Exercise 2-110:

Many more of these groupings are discussed in *THE RHYTHM BOOK—Crossrhythms on 4/4*.

Triplet Eighth Exercises

Here are some triplet-eighth-note exercises for you to practice, some of them with pickups and ties.

Exercise 2-111:

Exercise 2-112:

Exercise 2-113:

Exercise 2-114:

Exercise 2-115:

Exercise 2-116:

Exercise 2-117:

Practice transcribing triplet-eighth-note examples using Worksheet 2-W-020.

Triplet Eighths with Pitches

So far, we have looked at triplet-eighth exercises written in rhythmic notation. If you have been finding these difficult, make up more of them for yourself. Now, we add pitches. Try to play some of the following exercises by singing them, and some by playing them on your instrument (if you are an instrumentalist rather than a vocalist). If you are a drummer, try singing the pitches to develop these musical skills.

Exercise 2-118:

Exercise 2-119:

Exercise 2-120:

Exercise 2-121:

Exercise 2-122:

Exercise 2-123:

Multi-part Triplet Eighth Exercises

Finally, we try some multi-part triplet exercises you can do with others, with singing or clapping parts, or playing them on instruments.

Exercise 2-124:

Exercise 2-125:

With the next exercise, either play the parts on percussion instruments or do them on pitched instruments, improvising the pitches as you'd like, but playing the written rhythms:

Exercise 2-126:

Practice transcribing multi-part triplet-eighth-note examples using Worksheet 2-W-021.

How to Write Triplets That Begin on Off-Beats

Students have asked me questions like: "I'm transcribing a Bill Evans solo in which he plays triplet quarter notes that begin on an off-beat (for example, the "and of one")—how should I write that?"

The first thing that comes to my mind when I hear a question like this is "Do you really mean the 'and of one' in a straight eighth note sense, or is he swinging the eighth notes?" Either can be notated, but they look quite different.

By far, the more common case when I hear a question like this is that it turns out the eighth notes are swung. With swing eighth notes, the key is to realize that what you think of as the "and of one" in the measure:

Example 2-075:

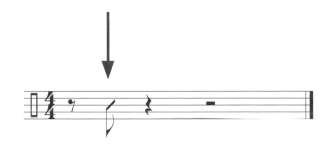

… is falling (at least approximately) on the third triplet of the beat:

Example 2-076:

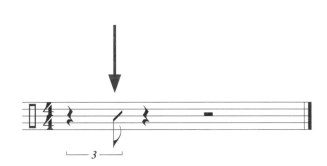

Since each triplet quarter takes as long as two triplet eighth notes, think how this is falling with respect to every triplet eighth note:

Example 2-077:

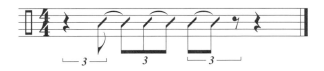

… and then simplify (assuming this is not a slow tempo with extremely precise duration of sustain necessary, I simplify the last note to a quarter note, rather than a triplet quarter note plus triplet eighth rest):

Example 2-078:

For the sake of thoroughness, I will address the other possibility—that you want to notate triplet quarter notes displaced by a straight eighth note—but this requires your familiarity with triplet 16th notes, which we have not yet discussed. This is discussed later in the book after we review triplet 16ths.

Changing Rate of Notes Within a Phrase

Much of the time, we find music is largely at one level of division (so, for example, we find much bebop at eighth-note level with occasional triplet eighths, and much funk at 16th-note level). However, the level of division can change within a passage, or even within a bar. Many people find that, at least at first, this change of rates can make it more challenging to sight-read the rhythms, even if the individual figures are ones they have no difficulty reading.

A comment to those of you who are teaching this material: I have found many teachers are strongly tempted to change the rate of notes very often in examples, even examples that they give to students who are just beginning to study rhythms. My suggestion: do not do this too early in the process! It's true that it can feel satisfyingly difficult to change between triplet eighths, eighths, 16ths, and even triplet 16th notes within a bar or two. The teacher can also feel this will sensitize the student to the way the different rates feel, even if these examples change rates more frequently than the vast majority of music one will come across in real life. My rule of thumb is that the student must be excellent and consistent at correctly notating rhythms at each of these rates before I start giving them any examples that change rates within the example.

There are two different approaches that you can use in reading music where the rate of division changes (and this refers to how you approach this internally, it will not be apparent to someone listening to you reading the music). One is to feel a different rate of underlying pulse as the rate of division in the rhythmic figures changes. For example, with the following, you might feel under the rhythms the pulses shown beneath the figures:

Example 2-079:

The benefit of this approach is that it can help in feeling the different rates of division in the rhythm figures; the cost is that it takes some extra effort to keep track of the different division of pulse that one feels in each bar (in the above example, it is almost like playing two simultaneous rhythm parts: the stem-down pulses and the stem-up rhythm figures). For many readers, it may prove to be a useful approach in learning to read music whose rate of division changes, but one you can abandon when you have more experience.

The other approach is to feel a constant pulse beneath the figures, feeling the figures divide this pulse differently:

Example 2-080:

Here is an example in which we change between quarter-note, eighth-note, and 16th-note levels:

Example 2-081:

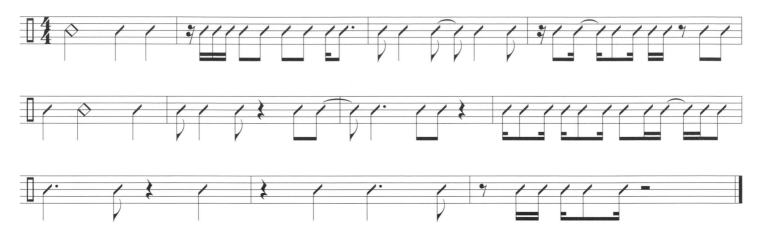

Try playing the above example in three different ways: first, play it all straight feel (straight eighth note, straight 16th note, etc.). Next, play it where you swing at the eighth-note level, but play straight (funk-like) when there are passages at the 16th-note level (so, for example, the second and third beats of the second bar are played straight eighth feel since they appear in the middle of a 16th-note phrase; but the fourth beat of the fourth bar is played with swing eighth feel because it is the pickup to a passage that is not 16th level). Finally, play it where you swing at each level you get to—i.e., when there are eighth notes, swing at eighth-note level but, where there are 16th notes, swing at the 16th-note level.

Here are some exercises to practice reading rhythms in which the level of division changes. The first changes between different triplet rates:

Exercise 2-127:

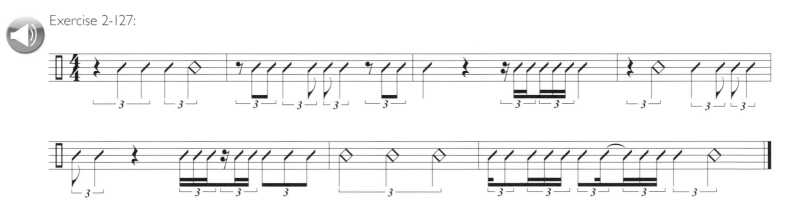

... and an exercise that is rhythmically the same as the previous exercise, but with pitches added:

Exercise 2-128:

Next, an exercise that changes between 16th notes and triplet eighth notes:

Exercise 2-129:

… and an exercise that is identical rhythmically but with pitches added:

Exercise 2-130:

Here, we change between both duple and triple divisions at different rates:

Exercise 2-131:

… and the following is rhythmically identical to the previous exercise, but adding pitches to it:

Exercise 2-132:

Practice transcribing examples in which the "grid" changes using Worksheet 2-W-022.

Feeling the Change in Grid—and Being Aware When It Does Not Change

Next, we will focus specifically on distinguishing 16th-note figures and triplet-eighth-note figures. First, however, I want to share a general observation. It is helpful to develop sensitivity to how different rates of pulse feel—and to develop an awareness of when a change in feel should alert you to a change in the rate of notes (the "grid," for example, if figures are at a 16th and triplet-eighth rate)—and, when there is no such change of feel (and the grid stays constant). A common mistake I see in people who are not very experienced with transcribing rhythms is that they write as though the rate of notes is changing when it is not. For example, with something that is clearly all on a triplet eighth grid:

Example 2 082:

They will write something with a changing grid, such as:

Example 2-083:

I think this is often due to unfamiliarity or lack of comfort with some common figures at different note rates. For example, in the incorrect Example 2-083, the person writing it was unfamiliar with the figure on beats "1" and "4." Although at a fast tempo, the distinction between Example 2-082 and Example 2-083 may not be large, to actually sound like Example 2-083, there would be a whipping back and forth feeling between a 16th grid on "1" and "4" and a triplet eighth grid on "2" and "3."

So, the general rule of thumb here is: "Do not change the rate of notes at which you are writing figures unless you really hear this change in rate."

Distinguishing Between 16th and Triplet-Eighth Figures

Now we examine a specific problem that some people encounter when they first begin to practice transcribing 16th and triplet-eighth rhythms: confusing figures that have some similarity, and thinking that the "grid" has changed when it has not.

A good way to overcome this is to specifically work on exercises that are as similar as possible between these rates, in order to both familiarize yourself with the figures and fine-tune your awareness of the distinctions.

First, we look at a triplet eighth note exercise:

Exercise 2-133:

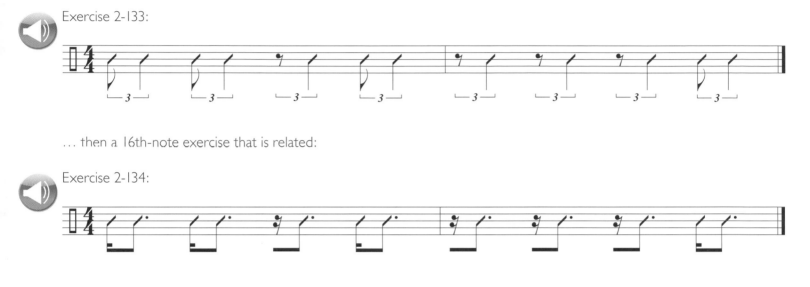

... then a 16th-note exercise that is related:

Exercise 2-134:

Similarly, the next few pairs of exercises have a triplet-eighth-based exercise first, followed by a related 16th-note exercise:

Exercise 2-135:

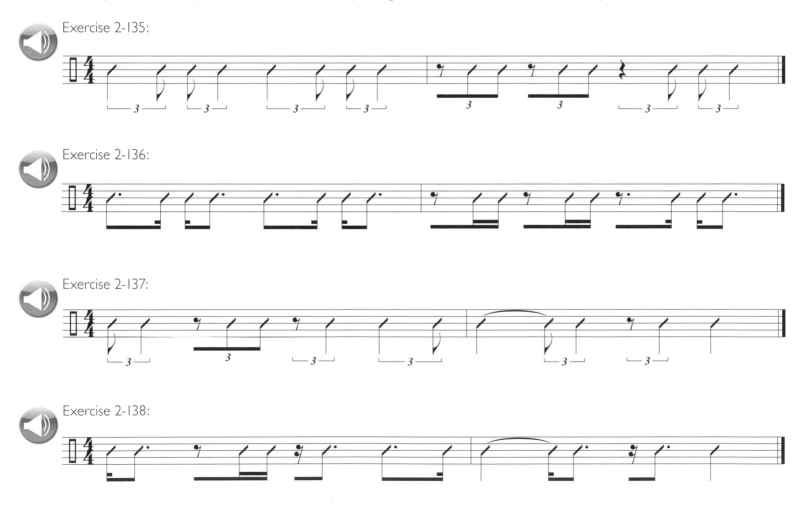

Exercise 2-136:

Exercise 2-137:

Exercise 2-138:

Exercise 2-139:

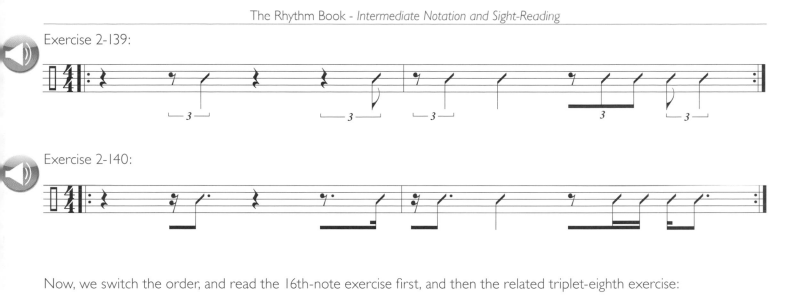

Exercise 2-140:

Now, we switch the order, and read the 16th-note exercise first, and then the related triplet-eighth exercise:

Exercise 2-141:

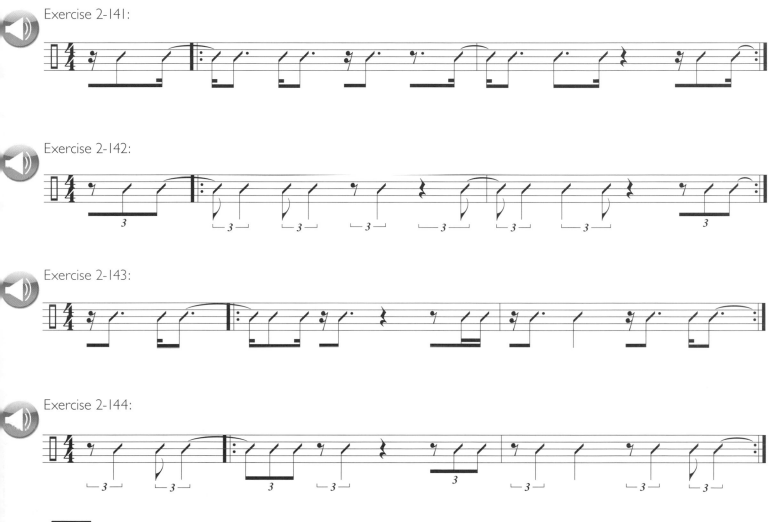

Exercise 2-142:

Exercise 2-143:

Exercise 2-144:

 Transcribe the examples on Worksheets 2-W-023 and 2-W-024 in order to develop your skills at distinguishing triplet-eighth and 16th figures.

How to Apply Notation Principles

Since we are discussing changes in the "grid"—the rate of notes within the measure—a question arises regarding the "required beats" to show in a bar. Here is a good general rule: find the finest division of the time that occurs within a measure, and show the required beats appropriate to that division. Note: There are other styles of notation that examine beat-by-beat rather than measure-by-measure; please see Appendix VI.

In 4/4, with duple divisions of the beat, here are the required beats to show: Quarter-note level: beat "one;" Eighth-note level: beats "one" and "three;" 16th-note level: every quarter note; 32nd-note level: every eighth note; 64th-note level: every 16th note; etc. With triple divisions of the beat, required beats are those for the next faster duple division; Triplet half notes: required beats for quarter notes (beat "one"); triplet quarter notes: required beats for eighth notes ("one" and "three"); triplet eighth notes: required beats for 16th notes (every quarter note); etc.

There are a couple places where exceptions to this are common and reasonable. One is when the "faster grid" is just an ornamentation or embellishment, so that the slower grid is really what one feels while reading it. For example, although the grace notes in the following example are written as 16th notes, the measure is really felt on an eighth-note grid, so it is sufficient to show "one" and "three" and write the last two beats as they are written here:

Example 2-084:

… rather than showing every beat, as a 16th note level example would have required:

Example 2-085:

The other place where we can violate the rule with no bad effects is when there are rests, for example, at the end of the bar. It is not necessary to write the last two beats as two quarter note rests:

Example 2-086:

There is no problem writing them instead as a half note rest. The person reading knows they will not play anything until the next measure, so they have no problem with not seeing each beat of rest.

Example 2-087:

Appropriate Level of Precision Revisited

There are several kinds of "overly precise" notation, especially in the context of jazz and other improvised music, which are to be avoided. The key point is that, in all of these examples, you could write the rhythms more simply and still with sufficient precision to get the results you want.

Unnecessary Precision in Showing "Swing"

It is useful and sometimes important to consider the performers for whom you are writing. It is possible that, on a rare occasion, you may find yourself writing for musicians who do not stylistically understand "swing" feel—for example, for a classical string section— and need to try to convey "swing" explicitly in your rhythmic notation. But, much more commonly, we see the opposite problem: inexperienced writers try to do this when they write for musicians who would provide the desired phrasing if they read much simpler notation accompanied by the "swing" symbol in parentheses.

Compare this more complex-looking attempt to explicitly show the swing:

Example 2-088:

... to this much simpler notation:

Example 2-089:

Unnecessary Precision in Note Duration

Avoid being more precise than necessary about note duration, especially with regard to short notes. Remember, unless you can tell the difference between the sound of two ways to notate a passage, choose the one that is easier to read. For example, we have seen the power of the staccato mark in simplifying notation. Especially at fast tempos, I have seen short notes written like the note on beat three in this passage (this example uses rhythmic elements we have not discussed and is a bit extreme, but just look at how much more is written!):

Example 2-090:

... where a much simpler version would sound the same:

Example 2-091:

Failure to Use "Behind the Beat" or "Ahead of the Beat"

In improvised music, a soloist may use relationship to the beat as a stylistic element, or a way to create tension and release. Often, if a passage is played slightly ahead or behind the beat, rather than notating it with extreme "metronomic" precision, (which requires more difficult-to-read rhythmic elements we have not yet discussed):

Example 2-092:

… if you understand the intent of the soloist and simply use terms such as "behind the beat" or "ahead of the beat," you can convey what the soloist is playing without making the notation difficult to read:

Example 2-093:

In jazz, notated rhythms are only an approximation of the rhythms as they are actually played, and you need to use good judgment in deciding how close an approximation is necessary for your purpose. The interpretive elements of swing, combined with relationship to the beat, may produce a passage that, if strictly metronomically transcribed, would be written:

Example 2-094:

… where, in fact, the soloist was not conveying septuplets (another more advanced rhythmic element we have not yet discussed) at all, and the passage could best be written:

Example 2-095:

Checklist and Correcting Notation

Now that we have discussed all the principles of notation needed to write music at the eighth, 16th, and triplet-eighth note levels, you can practice applying them by correcting the poorly notated examples on Worksheet 2-W-025 and, for each of them, describe the principle(s) violated.

You can also use a sort of mental checklist to make sure you have written something in the best way possible—notating rhythms well will become second nature to you as you do it more, and you will no longer have to consciously think of this checklist, but it can help at first:

- Did I accurately capture the rhythm I'm trying to write?
- Did I show the required beats? (At eighth note level in 4/4, did I show "one" and "three?" i.e. does it look like two well-notated bars of 2/4, but with the bar line between them removed? At 16th-note level, did I show each beat?)
- Did I avoid showing unrequired beats unnecessarily (at eighth-note level in 4/4, are the only ties I have ties into "one" and "three;" at 16th-note level, am I never tying any 16th notes within a beat)?
- Did I beam notes correctly? (Are all eighth notes that are part of the same beat beamed together? Did I avoid beaming into beat "three?")
- Did I write things at an appropriate level of precision? Did I use the "swing" symbol, or the expression "behind the beat," etc. where useful?
- Did I use the staccato mark where possible to simplify notation without changing the sound?

When your answer to all these questions is "yes," you know you have done all you need to in order to write a rhythm well.

16th-Note Triplets

We've looked at rhythms at the triplet half-note, triplet quarter-note, and triplet eighth-note levels; now we consider triplet 16th-note rhythms.

Introduction to 16th-Note Triplets

Eighth-note triplets are grouped to show what happens per beat, so you might logically expect 16th-note triplets to be written to show what happens per eighth note. In fact, at first, that is exactly what we will look at.

There are the same number of triplet-16th figures per eighth note as there were triplet-eighth figures per quarter note, and they are identical, except that they are twice as fast:

Example 2-096:

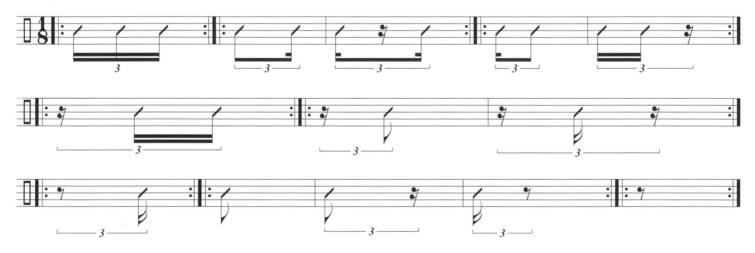

When written so that these figures replace some eighth notes in 4/4, we get music that looks like this (notice that we beam by beat, but do "secondary beaming" to separate the two halves of the beat):

Example 2-097:

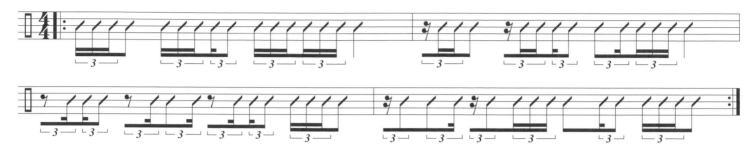

The following example features the same relatively small number of triplet-16th rhythms, but I have put them together in a way that perhaps you may find more challenging (especially the last two bars):

Example 2-098:

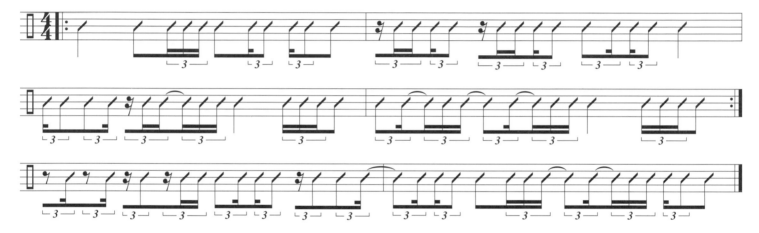

Perhaps even more challenging is the use of more space and more ties:

Example 2-099:

… but be sure to also be very comfortable with triplet 16ths when used like this (notice that I have incorporated some other rates in the example):

Example 2-100:

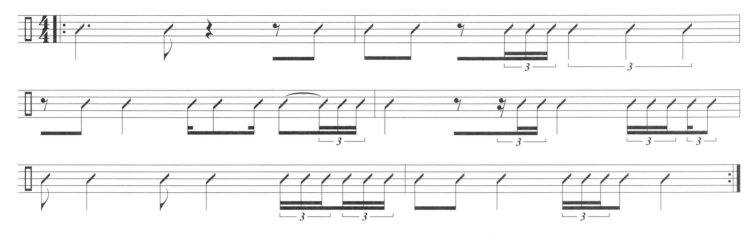

Write your own exercises, combining these triplet-16th figures in different ways, and try to challenge yourself. Practice them as you have previously practiced figures at other rates.

If triplet 16th notes were always written in this way (showing what happens on each eighth note), there would not be much more for us to discuss about them. However, 16th-note triplets are often written to show what happens per beat (i.e. per quarter note), rather than what happens per eighth note. The beat is felt in three different ways: 1) as a single unit divided into six equal parts; 2) as two eighth notes, each divided into three equal parts (i.e. how we divided it above); and 3) as three triplet eighth notes, each divided into two equal parts:

Example 2-101:

… which might most commonly be notated this way:

Example 2-102:

In the first bar, the "6" means 6:4 (six notes in the time of four). Squeezing music that lasts six 16ths into the time of four 16ths, or squeezing music that lasts three eighths into the time of two eighths, both produce the same result. These are different ways of expressing exactly the same superimposition, and all three bars sounds the same. However, when we use the "6," we typically call these "sextuplets." Notice that, in the second bar, each "3" only applies to the three 16th notes above it, while in the third bar, the "3" applies to the entire beat.

Because of these different ways of feeling and writing the same figure, there are many more ways triplet-16th figures may be written, and therefore quite a few of them to learn.

One approach we could use would be to write and learn every figure showing each of these three divisions. Using a couple figures as examples, we could write:

Example 2-103:

The benefit of this approach is that we could use it to create every possible notation for any figure. Notice that, if we include all the possible variations in how long the notes are sustained, it produces even more ways to write the same figure. For example, our first sextuplet above could be written in all of these ways:

Example 2-104:

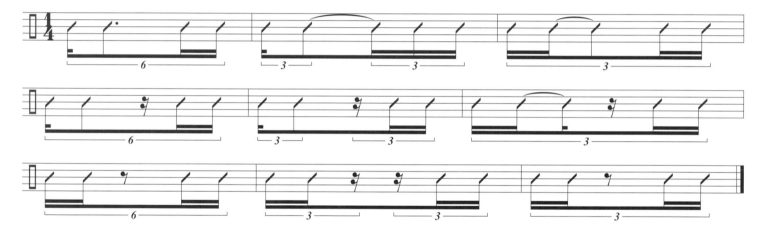

... and, our second figure could be written:

Example 2-105:

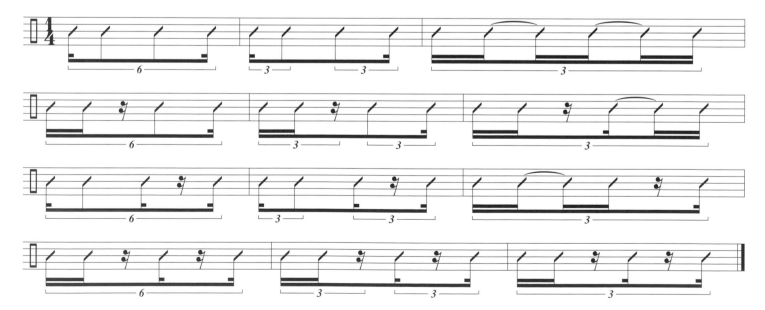

While you may think it would feel satisfying to see every way these figures can possibly be written, there are two problems with this approach. First, it produces an enormous number of variations necessary in order to show all of the triplet 16th-note figures, so there are a lot of them to learn. Second, many of them are ways we would rarely, if ever, write these figures in common practice. In common practice, we generally want to avoid showing unrequired beats (i.e., we do not have to show every 16th) and having ties within the beat, as it makes the music look unnecessarily "busy" and difficult to read. Therefore, writing every possible way in which these figures could be notated will result in many variations we should avoid.

Another approach we could use would be to pretend that every note in these figures can only last for a triplet 16th note. If we just make each entire beat a sextuplet, we could write:

Example 2-106:

etc...

The advantages of this are that there are fewer figures to write, it is easy to see each place a note can occur, we can just use the number "6," and we can avoid addressing the way the beat is divided. But the disadvantages are, if anything, greater. First, unless you are a drummer, you will almost never see music in which all notes are written short like this, and it is therefore a bad habit to write this way: We shouldn't write notes short if we want vocalists and instrumentalists to play them long. Second, thinking this way encourages you to write things that are far more difficult to read than necessary, and the opposite of common practice. For instance, in the previous example, the first measure is fine, but it would be much better to write the remaining three measures in this way (If you really wanted the notes to be as short as in the previous example, you could add staccato marks.):

Example 2-107:

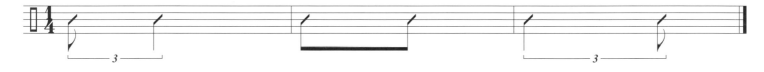

We can, however, use this idea to organize the figures.

Possibilities for Triplet 16th Notes per Beat

Now, let us look at all of the possible places that notes at the triplet 16th level can be played in a beat, and some of the most common ways to notate them. If you were going to only write rhythms and never read them, you could just learn and use a single way to notate each figure. But, others may use different notations, so you should be comfortable reading these common ways of writing the figures. Also, the context in which a figure occurs—the way the music in the preceding and following measures is felt—may influence which way you notate it.

> As you now understand, whether we write "3" (meaning three in the time of two) and call these triplet 16ths, or write a "6" (meaning six in the time of four) and call these sextuplet 16ths, they sound the same, and either is correct. The way you feel the beat—as one unit, or two eighth notes each divided into three, or three triplet eighths each divided into two—may dictate which you write. Also, you may find different people tend to use one or the other more, based on their musical backgrounds. For example, European classically trained musicians might more frequently use "6." I have used a mix of these so that you are familiar with each; where one way of feeling the beat seems most common, I've also let that influence my choice. Also, I will refer to notes at this rate as "triplet 16ths" rather than the more awkward and redundant "triplet 16ths and sextuplet 16ths."

In the following, within each set of repeat signs, I first show the figure with notes lasting only one triplet 16th note each (in most cases, this is *not* the way you should write it), and then some of the most common ways we might actually see the figure written:

Example 2-108:

One note per beat

Example 2-109:

Two notes per beat

Example 2-110:

Three notes per beat

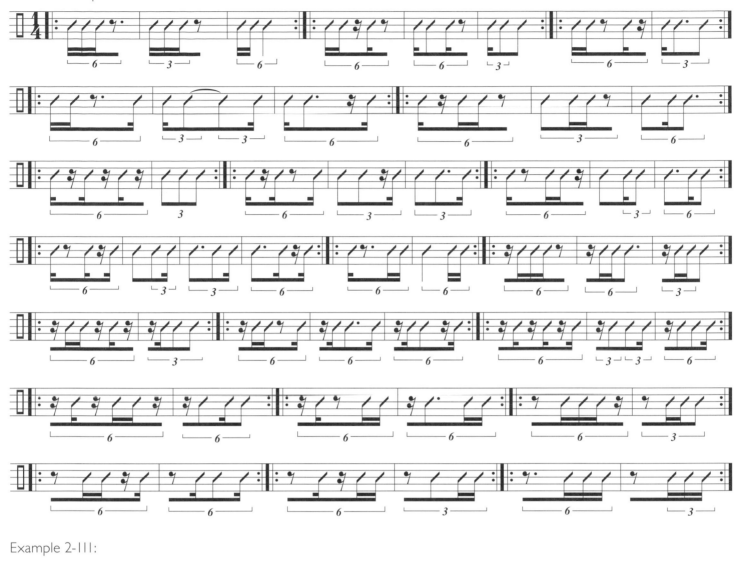

Example 2-111:

Four notes per beat

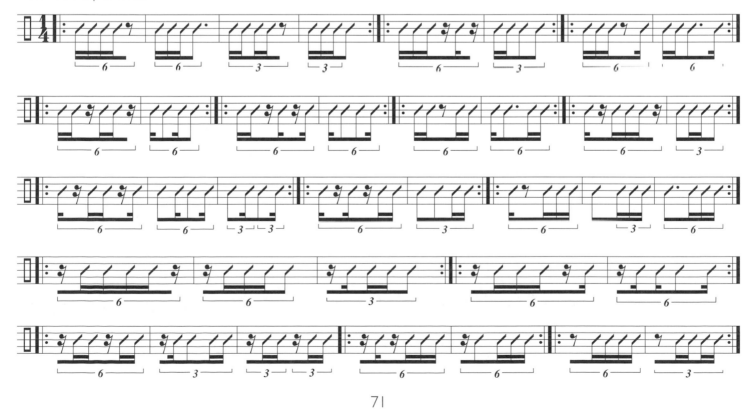

Example 2-112:

Five notes per beat

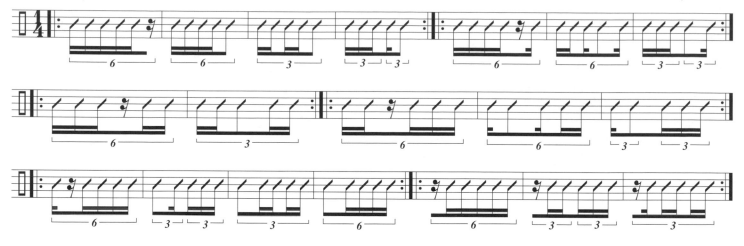

And, of course, the figure we looked at previously, in which all six notes are played:

Example 2-113:

Combinations

We can again systematically work on reading the figures with different numbers of notes per beat. As the figures with more notes per beat are often easier to read, and they may help you get into the 16th-note triplet groove better, I will proceed in these exercises from more notes per beat to fewer.

Combinations with five notes per beat:

Exercise 2-145:

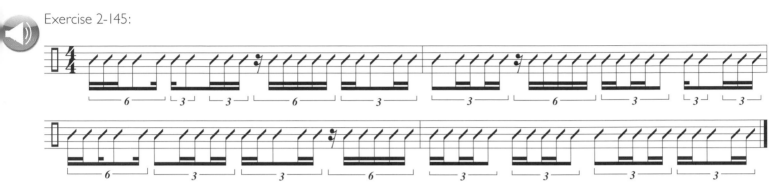

Combinations with four notes per beat:

Exercise 2-146:

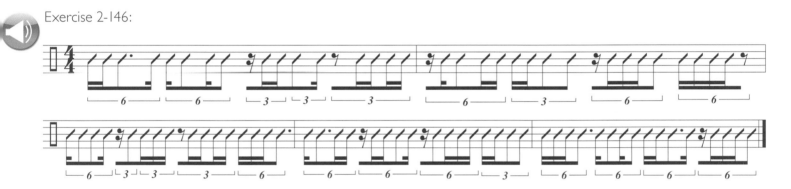

Combinations with three notes per beat:

Exercise 2-147:

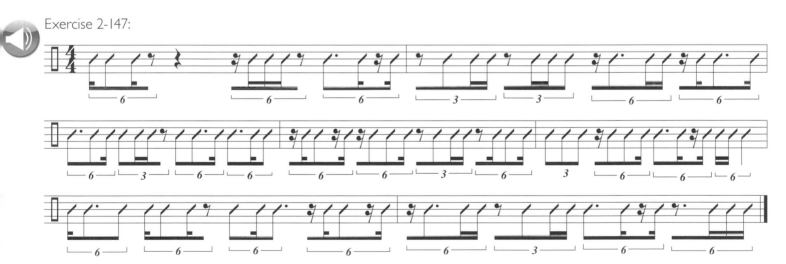

Combinations with two notes per beat:

Exercise 2-148:

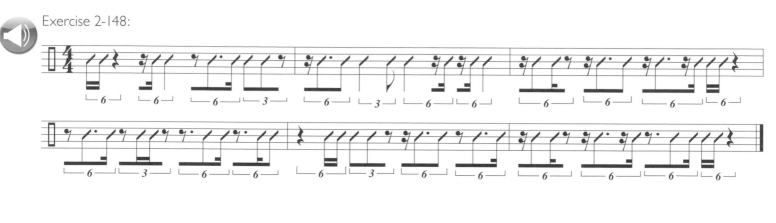

Combinations with one note per beat:

Exercise 2-149:

Notice that, if this exercise is straight eighth note feel, every time there is a dotted eighth rest followed by a 16th note and an eighth rest under the triplet sign, we could have written that beat without a triplet, with an eighth rest followed by an eighth note with staccato sign.

Now, we combine the figures with different numbers of notes per beat in the following exercises:

Exercise 2-150:

Exercise 2-151:

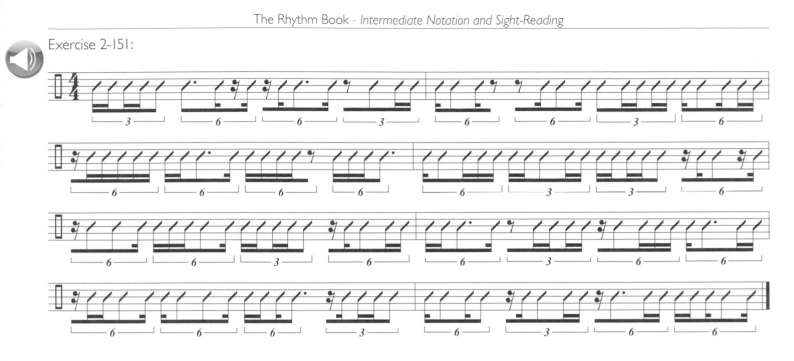

The following is the same as the previous exercise, but with some notes omitted:

Exercise 2-152:

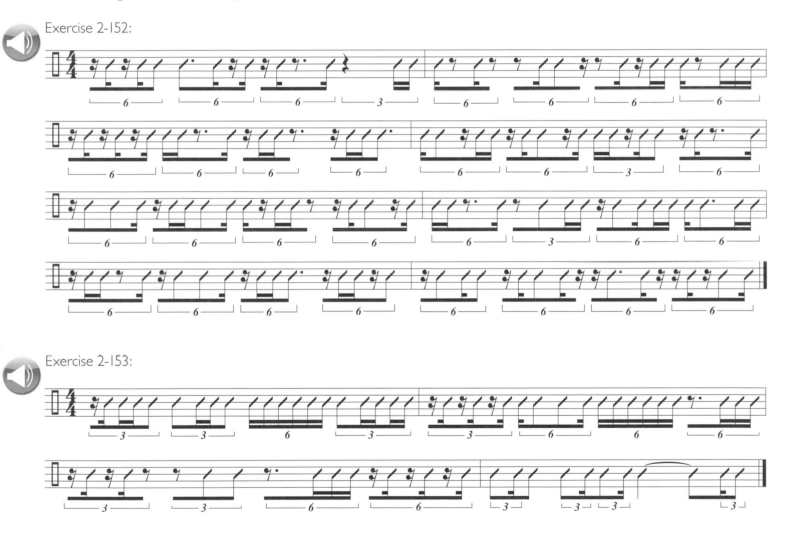

Exercise 2-153:

We will consider feeling each part of the 16th triplet, broken-16th triplets, and ties, groupings (crossrhythms) at the triplet-16th level, then work through some more exercises.

  Practice transcribing 16th triplets using Worksheet 2-W-026.

Feeling Each Part of the 16th Triplet

When we worked on eighth-note triplets, we practiced feeling each part of the beat. There are six triplet sixteenths per beat, so there are six places we need to be able to feel. Three of them we already addressed when we worked on triplet eighth notes:

Example 2-114:

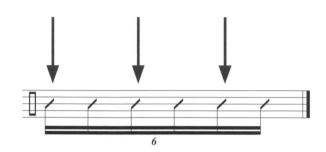

... and a fourth is familiar from our work on eighth notes (if we play the first and fourth of these triplet 16th notes, it sounds the same as playing two straight eighth notes):

Example 2-115:

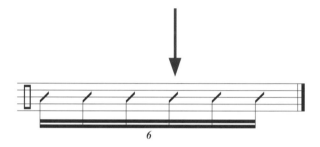

This leaves two new places with which we have to get comfortable, the second 16th:

Example 2-116:

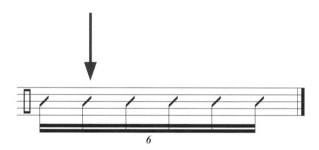

... which we can practice with this exercise (notice that, in this and the next several exercises, I've switched to showing beamed/half-stemmed rests, just so you get accustomed to another style of notation you may see):

Exercise 2-154:

… and the sixth 16th:

Example 2-117:

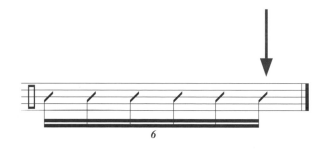

… which we can practice with this exercise:

Exercise 2-155:

"Broken" 16th Triplets and Ties

Once the 16th triplet figures are comfortable and familiar, we can practice exercises that incorporate ties with broken 16th triplets. In contrast to a steady stream of triplets, "broken triplets" is a term used to refer to breaking up the flow with sustained notes or rests, which produce syncopated triplet figures. For most people, broken triplets are a bit more challenging to read and write:

Exercise 2-156:

Exercise 2-157:

Exercise 2-158:

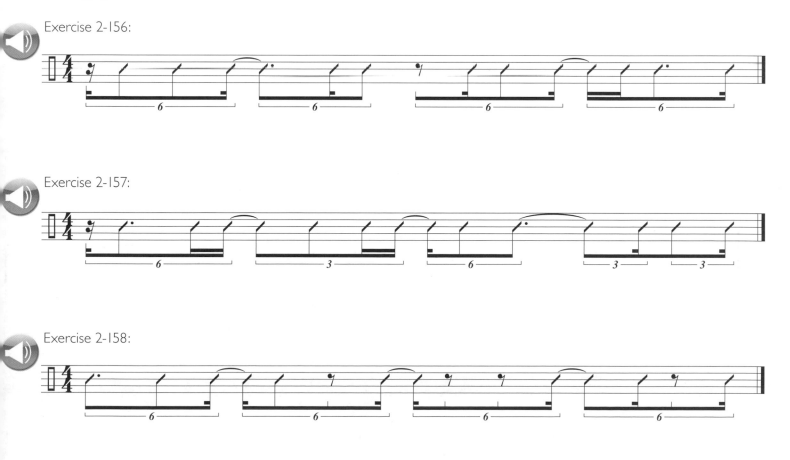

Exercise 2-159:

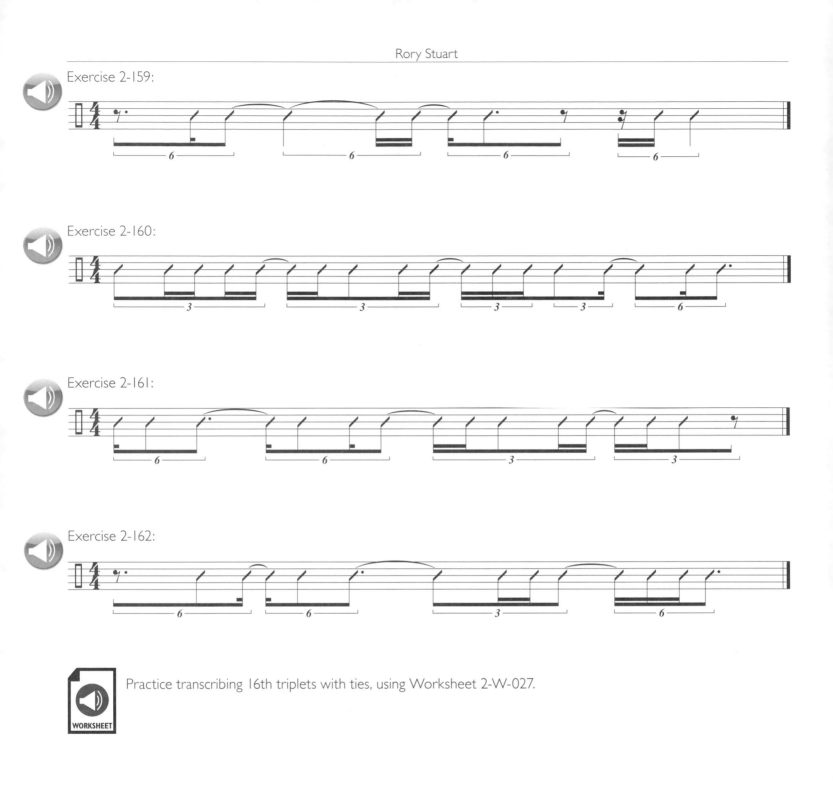

Exercise 2-160:

Exercise 2-161:

Exercise 2-162:

Practice transcribing 16th triplets with ties, using Worksheet 2-W-027.

Triplet 16th Groupings

Like playing triplet eighth notes in groupings, we can group triplet 16th patterns to imply crossrhythms. Here, we try a few exercises.

Triplet 16th notes grouped in fives:

Exercise 2-163:

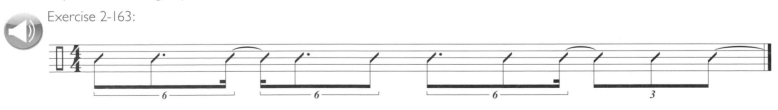

Triplet 16th notes grouped in sevens:

Exercise 2-164:

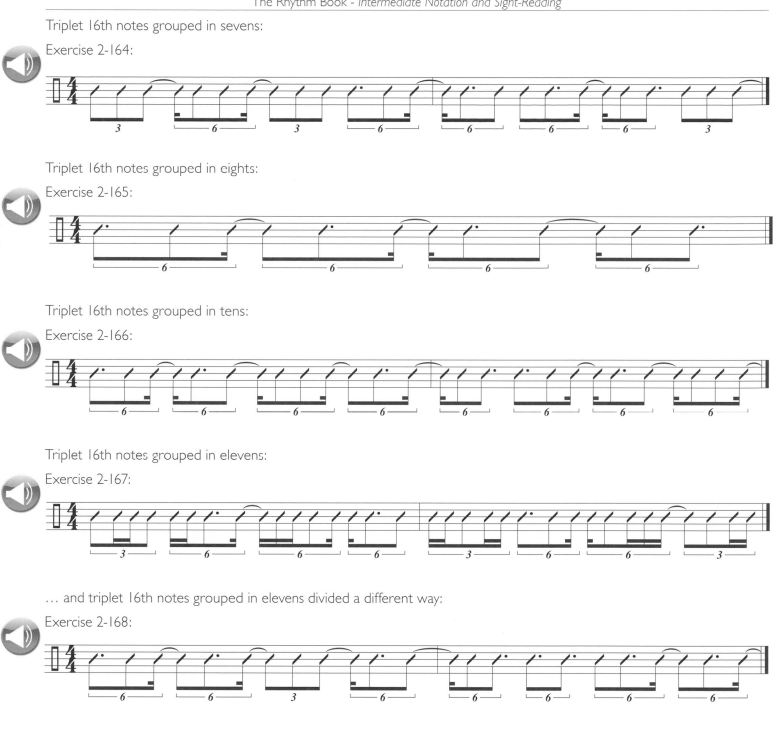

Triplet 16th notes grouped in eights:

Exercise 2-165:

Triplet 16th notes grouped in tens:

Exercise 2-166:

Triplet 16th notes grouped in elevens:

Exercise 2-167:

… and triplet 16th notes grouped in elevens divided a different way:

Exercise 2-168:

Notice in the previous exercise, in order to emphasize the grouping, I wrote the second bar all in triplet 16th notes. However, the second beat of the second bar could be more simply written as two eighth notes:

Example 2-118:

Practice transcribing 16th triplets grouped to imply crossrhythms, using Worksheet 2-W-028.

Triplet 16th Exercises

Here are some longer triplet 16th exercises, and some with pickups and ties.

Exercise 2-169:

Exercise 2-170:

Exercise 2-171:

Exercise 2-172:

Exercise 2-173:

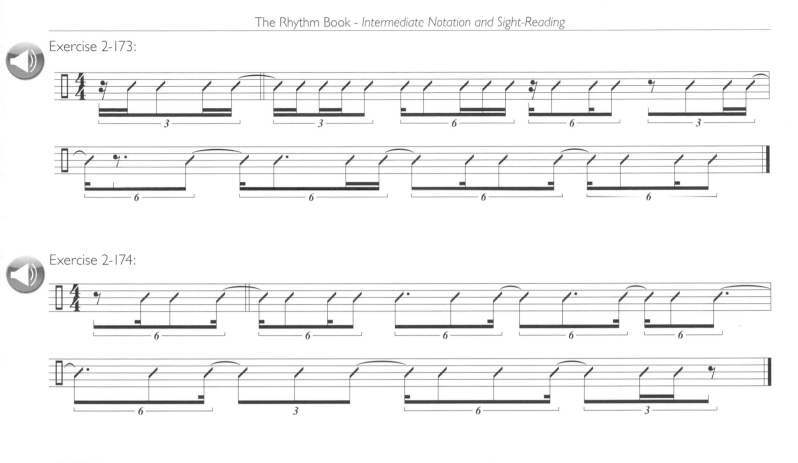

Exercise 2-174:

 Transcribe 16th triplets with pickups and ties, using Worksheet 2-W-029.

Triplet 16th Exercises with Pitches
Let's add pitches to the triplet 16th note reading.

The following exercise is the same as Exercise 2-153, but with pitches added:

Exercise 2-175:

Exercise 2-176:

Exercise 2-177:

Exercise 2-178:

Exercise 2-179:

Exercise 2-180:

 Practice transcribing 16th triplets with pitches, using Worksheet 2-W-030.

Multi-part Triplet 16th Exercises

Finally, some multi-part exercises you can do with others, with singing or clapping parts, or playing them on instruments.

Exercise 2-181:

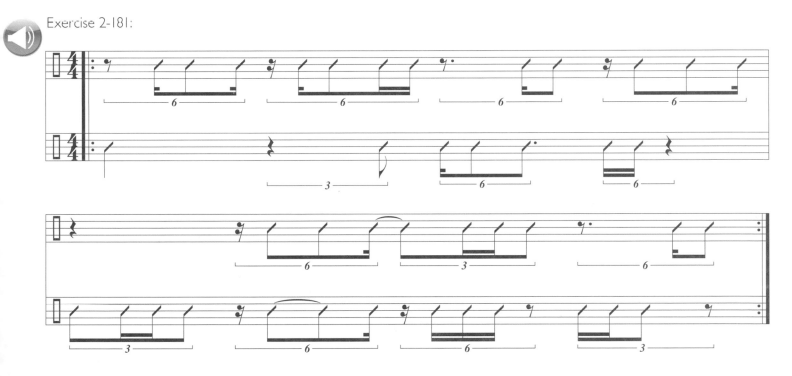

Exercise 2-182:

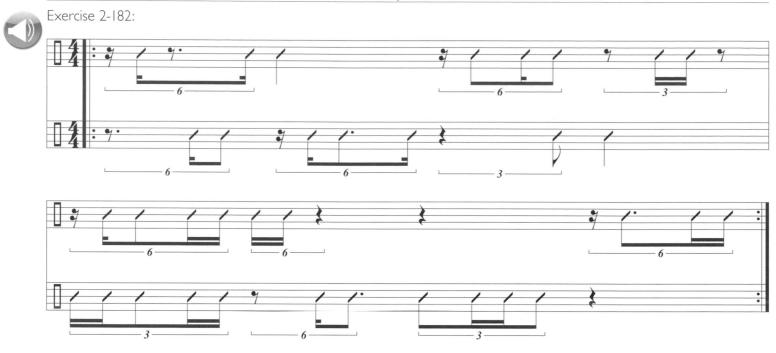

Exercise 2-183:

Exercise 2-184:

 Practice transcribing a multi-part 16th triplet example, using Worksheet 2-W-031.

How to Write Triplet Quarters and Eighths That Begin on Off-Beats in a Straight Eighth Context

We previously discussed when triplets begin on off-beats, but in a swing eighth context. Now that we have worked on triplet 16th notes, we can address the other case: triplets that begin on an off-beat in a straight eighth context.

Before you even consider this, be certain that this is really what you want to write—it is much more common for triplets to start on an off-beat in music with swing feel than in music with straight eighth note feel!

The insight you need here begins with recognizing the relationship between straight eighth notes and triplet 16ths. Notice that the figures on the first two beats sound the same:

Example 2-119:

straight eighth feel

We know that two triplet 16th notes tied together sound the same as one triplet eighth note. So, if we start tying together pairs of triplet 16th notes, starting, for example, on the "and" of one, we get this:

Example 2-120:

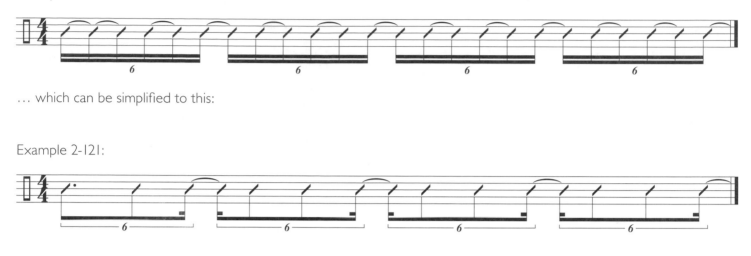

… which can be simplified to this:

Example 2-121:

Similarly, if for some reason we wanted to write triplet quarter notes starting on an off-beat in a straight eighth note context, for example, starting on the "and" of beat one, we would write:

Example 2-122:

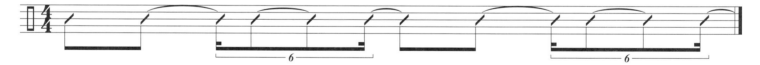

… which can be simplified to this:

Example 2-123:

32nd-Note Rhythms and Beyond

All the finer duple divisions of the beat may seem daunting, especially due to their unfamiliarity (it is rare to see these except in drum exercise books). But, at least in principle, they are easy, since they build on what we know already. Here, we review them briefly.

Introduction

Except for doubling double-time feel on ballads, transcription of very fast passages in solos, or occasional written flurries of notes in arrangements, it is not very often that we see figures written at 32nd-note rate, let alone 64th-note or 128th-note rates, at least not in a jazz context. However, we can apply the notation principles to any of these, and find that writing or reading them is quite similar to writing or reading music at the 16th-note level.

Notation of 32nd notes and 64th notes

At the 32nd-note level, the required beats to show are the eighth notes. The figures that can happen per eighth note are identical to the figures at the 16th-note level that could happen per beat, only twice as fast:

Example 2-124:

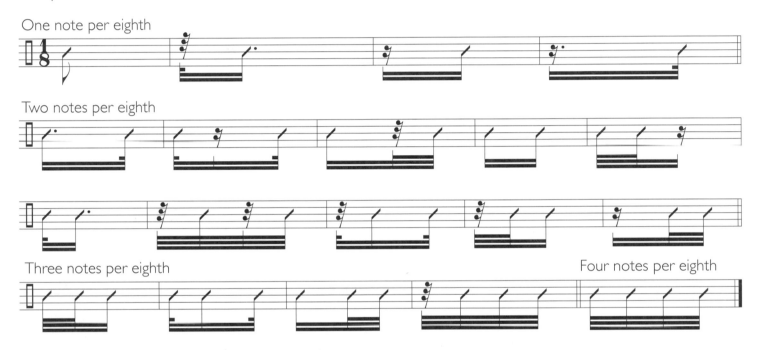

When we combine these figures, I strongly recommend a beaming scheme in which the entire beat is beamed together by a single beam, and then the finer divisions of each eighth note are beamed separately on top of this (this is called "secondary beams," although it is not essential that you know this!). Here is an example of one measure of 32nd-note level music written three ways, all "showing" the required beats. In the first way, rests are not beamed, and beats are not beamed together; in the second way, each beat is beamed together, but the beaming does not assist the reader's eye as well as it might to separate each eighth note in the last two beats; in the third way, which I recommend, the single beam helps the reader's eye group each beat, yet the finer divisions within each eighth note help the reader's eye distinguish which notes belong to each eighth:

Example 2-125:

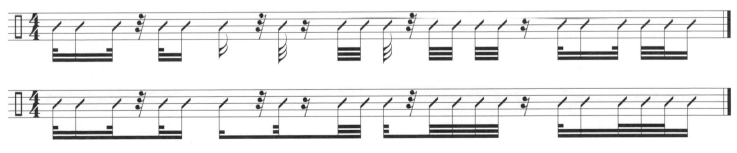

(this example continues on next page)

There is still one improvement we can make. By beaming the rest at the end of the third beat, and slightly modifying the secondary beaming, we can make each eighth note even more clear:

Example 2-126:

Here are some exercises combining 32nd-note figures:

Exercise 2-185:

Exercise 2-186:

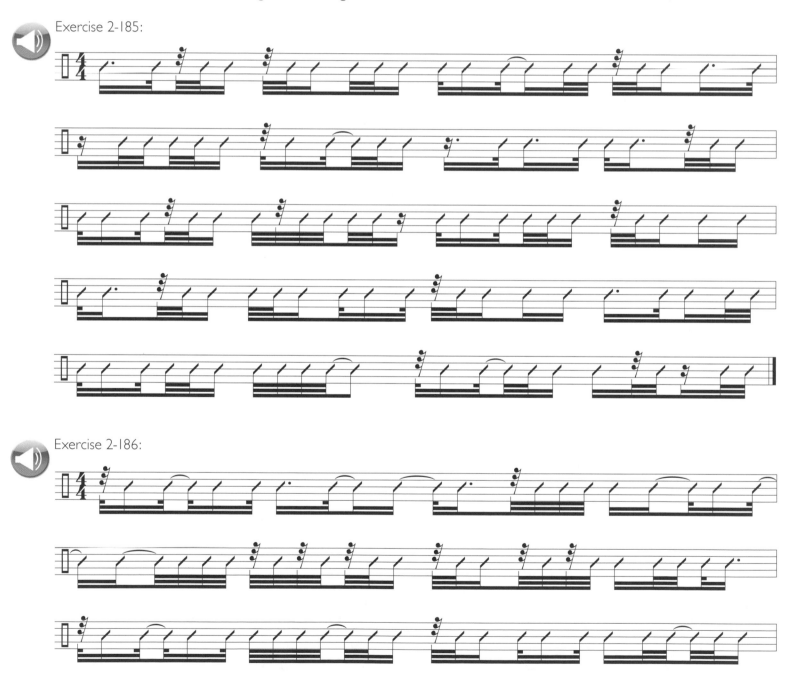

(this example continues on next page)

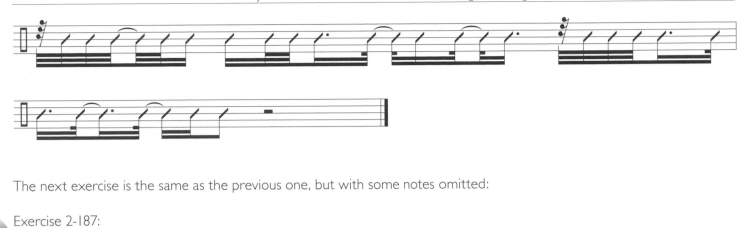

The next exercise is the same as the previous one, but with some notes omitted:

Exercise 2-187:

Exercise 2-188:

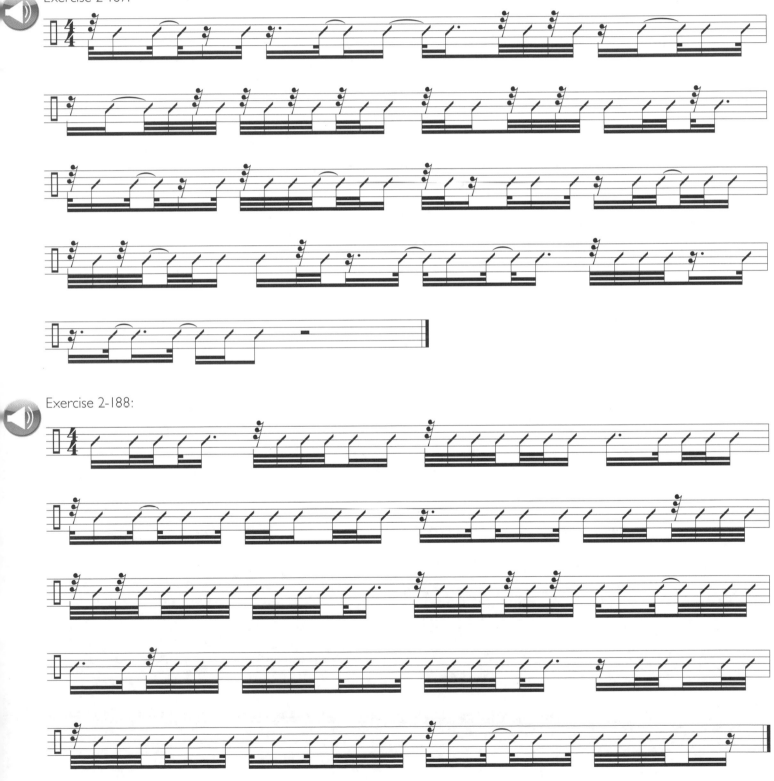

The next exercise is the same as the previous one, but with pitches added:

Exercise 2-189:

Although it is very rare to see 64th-note level music in a jazz context, let us look at this briefly. We will beam entire beats together with a single beam, but put all of the secondary beams at the finer level to help the reader's eye distinguish each 16th note within the beat. You can read 64th-note level music almost as though each beat is a bar of 4/4 in which you were reading four 16th-note figures. For example, look at the relationship between these four bars of 16th-note level music in 4/4:

Example 2-127:

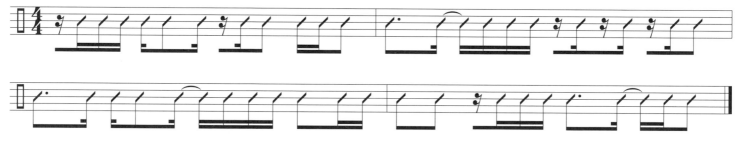

… and this one bar of 64th-note level music in 4/4:

Example 2-128:

Notice that the secondary beams should be broken to the 16th-note level in this case, to help the eye group each 16th-note phrase (and at the eighth-note level in the middle of each beat to help you see where the middle of each beat falls).

Here is another exercise at the 64th-note level:

Exercise 2-190:

While we may go a lifetime without running into 128th note music (not to mention 256th note, etc.), there is nothing new we need to learn in order to read it; we just follow the principles of required beats appropriate to each level. At the 64th level, the required beats to show were every 16th note, and we used secondary beaming so that we could see these within each quarter note. Similarly, with 128th note music, we would do the same, except showing each 32nd note.

Practice correcting poorly notated 32nd-note level examples, using Worksheet 2-W-032.
Practice transcribing 32nd-note level examples, using Worksheet 2-W-033.

Notation of 32nd-Note Triplets

Like 64th notes and 128th notes, we may rarely (if ever) come across 32nd-note triplets, but we want to be prepared to write or read them if necessary.

If we have music that is really 32nd note triplet-based, we can choose from one of two strategies. In the first strategy, we show each triplet eighth so that we see three of these 32nd-based figures (each the length of one of the triplet eighth notes) per beat:

Example 2-129:

In the second strategy, we show each eighth note so that we have six 32nd tuplets per eighth note:

Example 2-130:

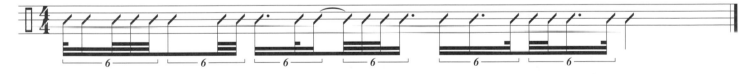

I think in most cases the first strategy results in something that is less difficult to read, so it is the one I recommend. But the feel of the music and the context (what happens immediately before and after) may dictate that one or the other is the better choice.

32nd and 64th Exercises

Here are some exercises that make use of 32nd notes, 32nd-note triplets, and 64th notes. Since these are rates you may rarely encounter, I've given you just a few representative exercises. You can easily create more of your own, for example, by writing 16th-note exercises twice as fast or four times as fast, or writing triplet 16th-note exercises twice as fast.

Here are a few exercises with 32nd notes:

Exercise 2-191:

Exercise 2-192:

… including one with pitches:

Exercise 2-193:

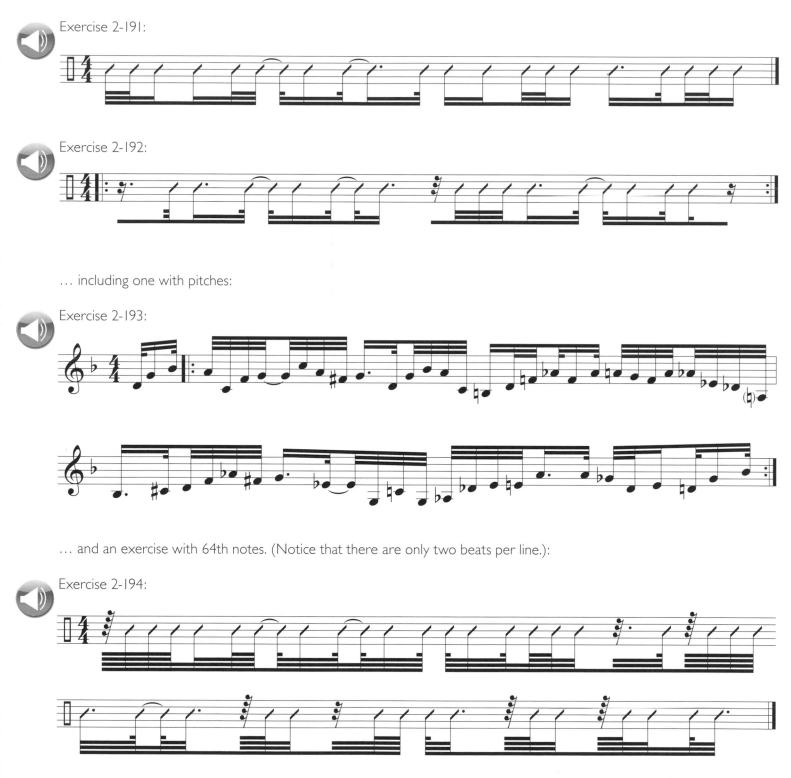

… and an exercise with 64th notes. (Notice that there are only two beats per line.):

Exercise 2-194:

… and a couple examples with 32nd-note triplets:

Exercise 2-195:

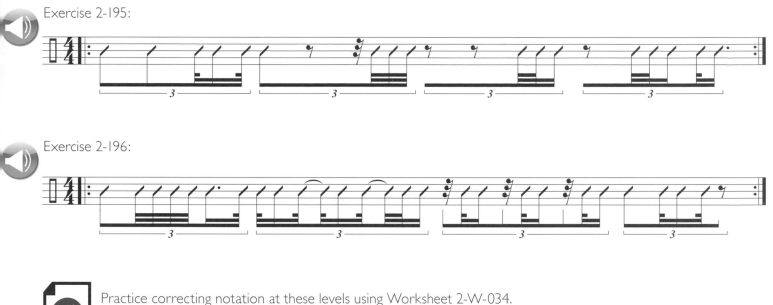

Exercise 2-196:

Practice correcting notation at these levels using Worksheet 2-W-034.
Transcribe examples of them using Worksheet 2-W-035.

Other Rates of Notes: Intro to Rhythmic Superimposition

There are rates of notes that are not divisions of two (i.e. not whole notes, half notes, quarter notes, eighth notes, 16th notes, 32nd notes, 64th notes). These notes at other rates are called rhythmic superimpositions and, in our work on triplets, we are already familiar with a simple example of a superimposition: the "3" in a triplet sign means we fit three of something in the time two would normally take.

There are many other rhythmic superimpositions possible, and we cover them in depth in *THE RHYTHM BOOK— Superimposition and Subdivision, Metric Modulation, Feel Modulation and Displacement*. For now, since we are looking at notation, I just want to touch on how these are written.

In the first two beats of the following example, there are five eighth notes and an indication, 5:4. This ratio, 5:4, tells us to squeeze five of these eighth notes in the time four would normally take. Four regular eighth notes would take two beats in 4/4 (two quarter notes).

Thus, it tells us to evenly play five notes during the first two beats of the measure.

Example 2-131:

5:4

For more about how rhythmic superimpositions, including how to sub-divide them and how to play them, see *THE RHYTHM BOOK—Superimposition and Subdivision, Metric Modulation, Feel Modulation and Displacement*.

Changing Tempo

There are five ways in which a change in tempo can be indicated. The first four of these are quite simple.

Accelerando and Ritardando

If the change in tempo is gradual rather than immediate, we can use the term "accelerando" (abbreviated accel.), which indicates to accelerate i.e. progressively speed up; or ritardando (abbreviated rit. or ritard.) which indicates to decelerate i.e. progressively slow down. There are some other terms used in classical music to indicate going to a faster tempo (e.g. "piu mosso") or to a slower tempo (e.g. rallentando, abbreviated rall.). To indicate a return to the previous tempo, we can use the terms "a tempo" or "tempo primo."

Example 2-132:

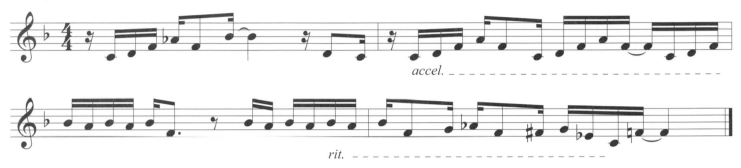

Tempo Descriptions

Verbal descriptions of tempos and feels can occur at the beginning of sections of a piece of music. This is found commonly in classical music, less commonly in some other styles. In the classical world, we might see expressions such as "allegro," "vivace," "lento," "andante," "presto," and many others. In other styles of music, we might find verbal descriptions such as "fast funk," "slow shuffle," "medium swing," or "bright samba." These describe a tempo/feel without reference to what came before it.

Example 2-133:

Metronome Markings

A very precise description of tempo (though not feel) can be expressed by indicating a metronome marking. Therefore, we can use metronome markings to indicate where the tempo changes and specify the new tempo.

A metronome marking shows a note value followed by an equal sign and then a number. The number indicates the tempo by telling us how many notes of that value will occur per minute. If a quarter note = 60 in one section, and quarter note = 180 in the next section, the latter section is three times faster than the former. Through our choice of note value, we can indicate the same thing in different ways. For example, if we wrote dotted half note = 60, that means 60 dotted half notes occur per minute, which is the same as saying 180 quarter notes occur per minute. Therefore, quarter note = 180 and dotted half note = 60 are two different ways of indicating the same tempo. Usually, we would choose the note value that is felt as the beat. In 4/4, we would generally show the metronome marking for a quarter note; in 11/8, the metronome marking for an eighth note.

Here is an example of using metronome markings to indicate change in tempo:

Example 2-134:

Tempo Relationship Descriptions

Rather than using the methods described above, we can use words to describe the relationship between one tempo and another. For example "double time" (sometimes abbreviated "dbl x") indicates that the new section should be played at twice as fast a tempo as the previous section. Other phrases of this type include "half time," "triple time," "quadruple time," etc., though by far the most commonly used are "half time" and "double time." Note that, with this method, the entire piece can be played faster or slower, but the relationship between tempos will remain the same. Tempo relationships can also be described less precisely, for example, "slightly faster."

Example 2-135:

Metric Modulation

When a tempo change happens instantly (as opposed to accelerando or ritardando), and there is a precise metric relationship between two tempos, we can use the notation for metric modulation. The notation for metric modulation shows the new tempo relative to the previous tempo, but it does so with note values.

A simple example, such as "double time" would be notated:

Example 2-136:

What this means is that, if we tap quarter notes in the first tempo and keep tapping at the same rate, what we are tapping will sound like half notes in the new tempo.

A big advantage of this notation over describing tempo relationships in words is that we can show things such as:

Example 2-137:

If we try to describe this in words, it is quite awkward. Any way we describe it ("four-thirds time," "one third faster," etc.) will be somewhat difficult to understand; but, expressed in metric modulation notation, it is clear and unambiguous.

There is a great deal more to consider in order to master the performance of metric modulations, and this topic is discussed in depth in *THE RHYTHM BOOK—Superimposition and Subdivision, Metric Modulation, Feel Modulation and Displacement*. For now, we know what we need to in order to correctly notate them.

Comparison of Ways to Indicate Tempo Change

In comparing the ways we've discussed to indicate tempo changes, we see these advantages and disadvantages of each:

• Accelerando and ritardando are the only ways to show a tempo that is changing gradually rather than instantly. By themselves they do not tell how fast or slow the tempo we arrive at should be, though they can be combined with a tempo description or metronome marking in order to do that.

• Tempo descriptions (such as "fast samba") are imprecise, but they can also convey information about feel and style.

• Metronome markings are very precise, though we have to compare them in order to notice any relationship between the previous and the new tempo. Do not assume that everyone who reads what you have written will immediately have the correct tempo in mind when they see your metronome marking.

• Tempo relationship descriptions (such as "double time") do not convey the absolute tempos but can convey the relationships in ways that even someone with little musical training can understand. However, they are awkward for expressing some precise relationships (such as "four thirds as fast").

• Like tempo relationship descriptions, metric modulation notation conveys the relationships between tempos, but not the absolute tempo. They require that the person reading them understand how they work (as compared to a description such as "double time"), but are a very clear way to express relationships that are awkward and unclear when put into words (such as ♩. = ♩).

Rhythms in Other Meters

So far, we have worked on writing and reading rhythms in 4/4 (with some examples in 2/4). In this section, we will look at how to read and write rhythms in other meters.

3/4

Introduction to 3/4

Other than 4/4, 3/4 is the meter we encounter most frequently in many styles of music. In jazz, this is a very comfortable and familiar meter for any experienced player. So, it is surprising to hear how stiff some early examples in the 1950s could sound. Fats Waller's "Jitterbug Waltz" from the early 1940s is a hip tune but, if you go back to the original recording (rather than more recent modern interpretations), it does not have the feel and flow that developed for 3/4 with John Coltrane's Quartet or the groups of Bill Evans. Similarly, "Valse Hot" with Max Roach and Clifford Brown (1956) has an element of "oom pah pah" in its original recording, even though it is being played by some of the hippest musicians of the time.

With our foundation in notating 4/4, notation in 3/4 is easy.

Notation in 3/4: Applying Notation Principles

The principles of rhythmic notation we've used in 4/4 give us a good head start in notating in other meters. In 3/4, at the quarter note level, we only have to show beat "I" and have no choice but to do so (so it's not a very useful rule!). We do not want to unnecessarily show the other beats. So, for example, do not write quarter note 3/4 music like this:

Example 2-138:

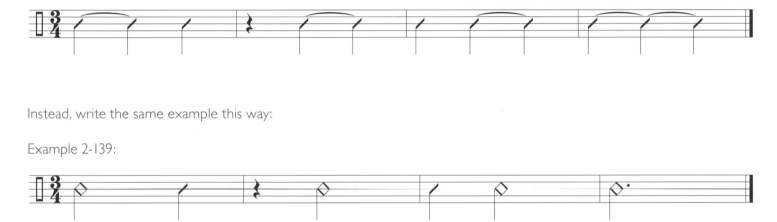

Instead, write the same example this way:

Example 2-139:

At the 16th-note level and beyond, the rules are exactly the same as in 4/4: at 16th-note level, show every quarter note (and, at 32nd-note level, show every eighth note, and so forth); and do not unnecessarily show unrequired beats.

Here is an example of poor 16th-note notation in 3/4 :

Example 2-140:

... and the same rhythm well-notated:

Example 2-141:

Did you catch my mistake? In the second bar, I beamed together three 16ths; it would be better here if the rests were included in the beams for each beat.

Here is a well-notated example that has pitches, is syncopated, and uses ties:

Example 2-142:

Thus, in 3/4, we only need to know additional rules when we are at the eighth-note level.

Let's look at some eighth note level 3/4 examples notated different ways, and think about which you prefer:

Example 2-143:

vs.

Example 2-144:

Which would you rather be given to read? What about the choice between the follow two examples?

Example 2-145:

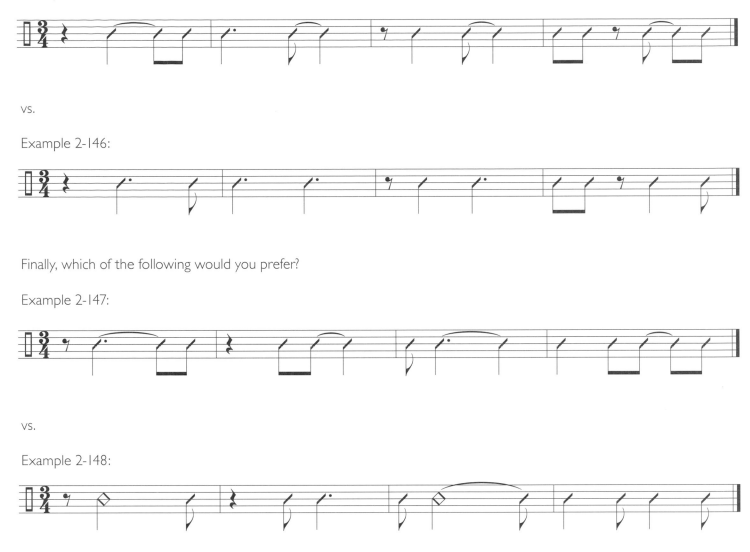

vs.

Example 2-146:

Finally, which of the following would you prefer?

Example 2-147:

vs.

Example 2-148:

In the above pairs of examples, the first version was written showing beats "1" and "3" while the second version was written showing "1" only. With almost all principles of notation we discuss, in almost every example, the "rules" we recommend consistently produce examples that are more easy and clear to read. But here, for the first time, we see two different rules ("show beats 1 and 3 when you write in 3/4 at the eighth note level" vs. "show only beat 1 when you write in 3/4 at the eighth note level") that produce similarly good results.

> I have shown eighth note examples in 3/4 written to show "1" and "3" or only to show "1" to many people and neither of the two ways of notating seems to receive a widespread preference. Which is preferred seems to depend on the audience and the particular example.

As an aside, here is one bar that, even if I generally only chose to show beat "1," I would not write this way:

Example 2-149:

... even if I were not showing beat "3," I would definitely choose:

Example 2-150:

Overall, my conclusion about writing eighth note music in 3/4 is that, because there are so few beats in 3/4, either way is easy to read. Therefore, you can either show beats "1" and "3" or just beat "1"—use whichever rule you prefer and you can feel confident people will be fine reading what you have written.

 Correct poorly notated 3/4 examples, using whichever rule you prefer, on Worksheet 2-W-036.

Here are a few exercises in 3/4.

> Since we have already worked on some tricky material in 4/4, including 32nds and 64ths, as well as triplet 16ths and 32nds, you may be surprised that we are returning to quarter, eighth, and 16th rhythms for these exercises. We return to these rhythm so that we can focus on the meter: on feeling, hearing, and seeing how rhythms fit in 3/4.

At the quarter-note level:

Exercise 2-197:

Exercise 2-198:

... at the eighth note level:

Exercise 2-199:

Exercise 2-200:

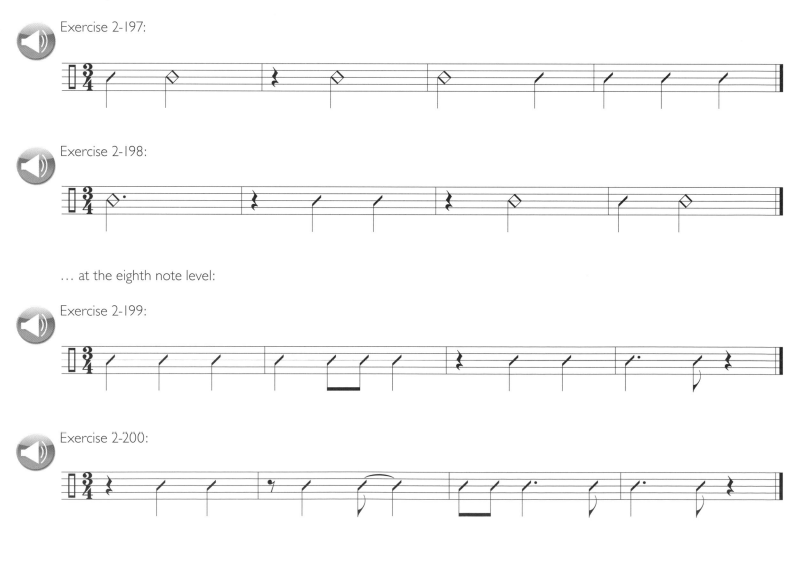

Exercise 2-201:

Exercise 2-202:

… and at the 16th-note level:

Exercise 2-203:

Exercise 2-204:

Exercise 2-205:

Transcribe 3/4 examples on Worksheet 2-W-037.

3/4 Feels

Although in this volume (and *THE RHYTHM BOOK—Beginning Notation and Sight-Reading*) our focus is on notation, you should be aware that there are a number of different feels that may be written in 3/4. This includes funk and 16th-note-based 3/4, and Afro-Cuban and Brazilian-based 3 feels. It also includes swing in 3/4 in which the emphasized pulse is dotted half notes (sometimes called "1" feel), or dotted quarter notes (for great examples of the latter, listen to many 3/4 performances by John Coltrane's Quartet with Elvin Jones on drums), or quarter notes ("3" feel). By the early 1960s, groups such as Coltrane's and the trios of Bill Evans had 3/4 firmly established in the jazz repertoire. For a thorough discussion of 3/4 styles, see *THE RHYTHM BOOK—Odd Meters and Changing Meters*.

Pickups in 3/4

Like pickups in 4/4, pickups in 3/4 are written without rests preceding them. The trick is simply to see where the pickup falls with respect to the count-off. Here we practice some 3/4 exercises with pickups:

Exercise 2-206:

Exercise 2-207:

Exercise 2-208:

Exercise 2-209:

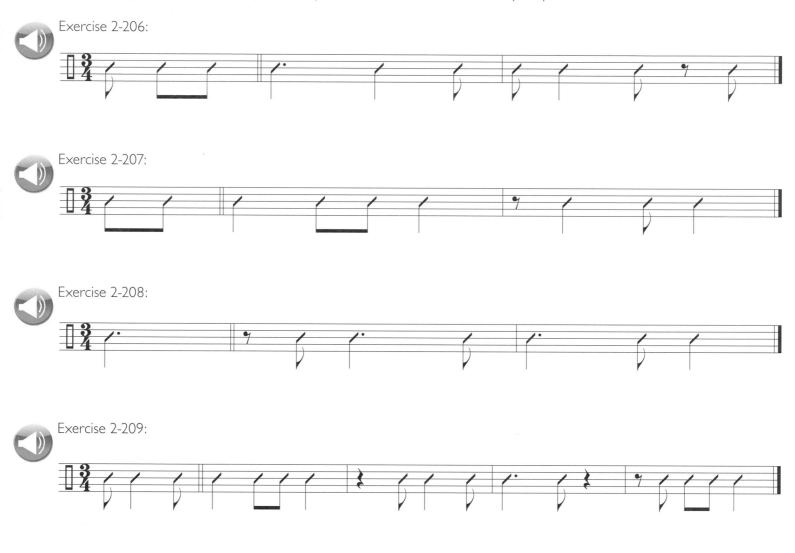

 Transcribe 3/4 examples with pickups on Worksheet 2-W-038.

102

Ties in 3/4

Practice these eighth-note-and 16th-note-based exercises in 3/4 with ties:

Exercise 2-210:

Exercise 2-211:

Exercise 2-212:

Exercise 2-213:

Exercise 2-214:

Exercise 2-215:

 Transcribe 3/4 examples with ties on Worksheet 2-W-039.

3/4 Exercises

Read these longer 3/4 exercises that use pickups and ties.

Exercise 2-216:

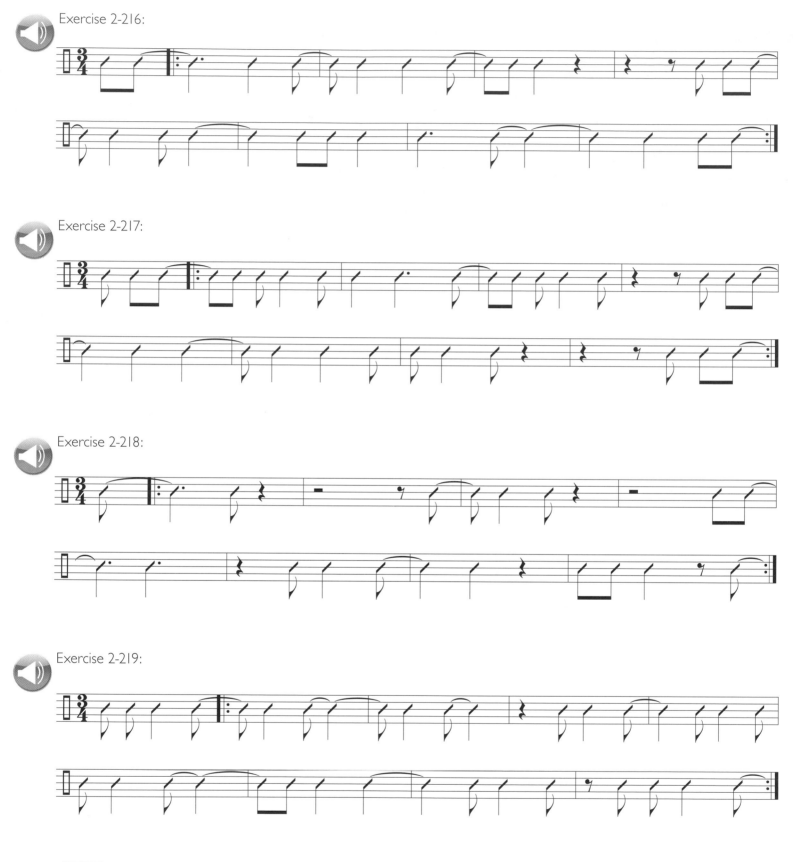

Exercise 2-217:

Exercise 2-218:

Exercise 2-219:

 Transcribe 3/4 examples like these on Worksheet 2-W-040.

3/4 Exercises with Pitch

Let's add pitches to our practice exercises in 3/4:

Exercise 2-220:

Exercise 2-221:

Exercise 2-222:

Exercise 2-223:

Multi-Part 3/4 Exercises

Finally, let's practice some multi-part exercises:

Exercise 2-224:

Exercise 2-225:

Exercise 2-226:

Transcribe multi-part 3/4 examples with ties on Worksheet 2-W-041.

More Advanced Rhythms in 3/4

Now that you have worked through the examples, exercises, and worksheets in this section, you should be comfortable feeling, reading, and notating rhythms in 3/4. You can create your own more advanced exercises using 32nds and 64ths, as well as triplet 16ths and 32nds. For example:

Example 2-151:

As you can see, reading these figures beat-by-beat is the same in 3/4 as in 4/4. The only additional challenge is feeling the 3/4 meter, a skill you've already developed by practicing eighth-note, triplet-eighth, and 16th-note exercises in 3/4.

Triple Meters
What is a Triple Meter?

There is one very distinctive type of meter that we have yet to consider: the triple meter. By "triple meter," I include frequently used meters such as 6/8, 9/8 and 12/8—but also 3/8, 15/8, 18/8, 21/8—any meter whose top number (i.e. numerator, to use the math term) is divisible by three, and whose bottom number (i.e. denominator, in math terminology) is "8." This special category of meter is sometimes called "compound meter" in the vocabulary of classical music, although that term has never made a lot of sense to me. (In what sense is it "compounded?") As we will see, triple meters are distinctive because of the note that is felt as the "beat" in a triple meter.

> It is important to be aware that I am using terminology in a somewhat different way than is typically used in classical music. Classical music theorists typically use "triple meter" to mean a meter that has three beats, and they contrast "compound meter" (a dotted quarter based meter, that I would describe as "triple meter") with "simple meter." Therefore, they would call 3/4 a "simple triple meter;" 6/8 a "compound duple meter" ("duple" because it has two beats); and 9/8 a "compound triple meter." They would call 12/8 a "compound quadruple meter." With no disrespect intended towards classical theorists, this is not the naming convention that I hear anyone use outside the classical world, nor one that seems to me to be especially useful in a practical sense. In the non-classical world "triple meter" is used to describe the dotted quarter-based meters such as 3/8, 6/8, 9/8, and 12/8, and that is the convention I use here.

6/8 vs 3/4

Let's look at a typical example of music written in 6/8:

Example 2-152:

Compare that to this example written in 3/4:

Example 2-153:

If you look only at the duration of each note, these two examples may seem similar to you. But musically, in terms of sound and feel, they are very different. In 3/4, we feel each quarter note as the underlying pulse; in 6/8, we feel dotted quarters as the pulse.

So, for example, the second bar of the previous examples, which feels very syncopated in 6/8, feels like an unsyncopated tapping of the pulse in 3/4.

This 6/8 example exemplifies the thing that is unique to triple meters, and that they share in common: the dotted quarter note pulse we feel, whether the meter is 3/8, 6/8, 9/8, 12/8, 15/8, 18/8, 21/8, etc.

Notation in Triple Meters

Given that the dotted quarter note is the pulse in triple meters, music in a triple meter should show the dotted quarter: make each dotted quarter visible, and beam by dotted quarter.

Let's contrast some poorly notated examples that violate principles of good rhythmic notation.

Here is a 6/8 example that is poorly notated because it fails to show required beats:

Example 2-154:

In order to correct it, look at what is happening dotted quarter by dotted quarter note—notice that I show each eighth note in the first bar, which is eighth note-based, and each 16th note in the second bar (because it is 16th-based):

Example 2-155:

… and then simplify (i.e. remove all cases where we unnecessarily show unrequired beats):

Example 2-156:

Here is a 6/8 example that is poorly notated because it is written as though it is in 3/4:

Example 2-157:

… and a well-notated version of the same example:

Example 2-158:

Here is a 6/8 example that fails to beam the notes together as they should be beamed:

Example 2-159:

… and the same example written with proper beaming by dotted quarter:

Example 2-160:

Here, the beaming has mistakenly crossed between the dotted quarters:

Example 2-161:

… and can be written correctly in this way:

Example 2-162:

 Practice correcting poorly notated examples in 6/8 using Worksheet 2-W-042.

Possible Figures Per Dotted Quarter

If we know what can happen per dotted quarter, we can combine these figures in different ways to produce all the possible rhythms in 6/8, 9/8, 12/8, and other triple meters. Here are the figures possible per dotted quarter at the eighth- and 16th-note levels, shown in some of the most common ways they are notated. I haven't included every variation in how long the notes are sustained, but repeat signs are used to show measures in which the onsets of notes are identical (it is up to you wheter you actuallly play the written repeats):

Example 2-163:

6/8 Exercises

Here are some exercises to practice 6/8:

Exercise 2-227:

Exercise 2-228:

Exercise 2-229:

Exercise 2-230:

Exercise 2-231:

Exercise 2-232:

Exercise 2-233:

... and some exercises in 6/8 with pickups:

Exercise 2-234:

Exercise 2-235:

Exercise 2-236:

Exercise 2-237:

Exercise 2-238:

... and some with ties:

Exercise 2-239:

Exercise 2-240:

Exercise 2-241:

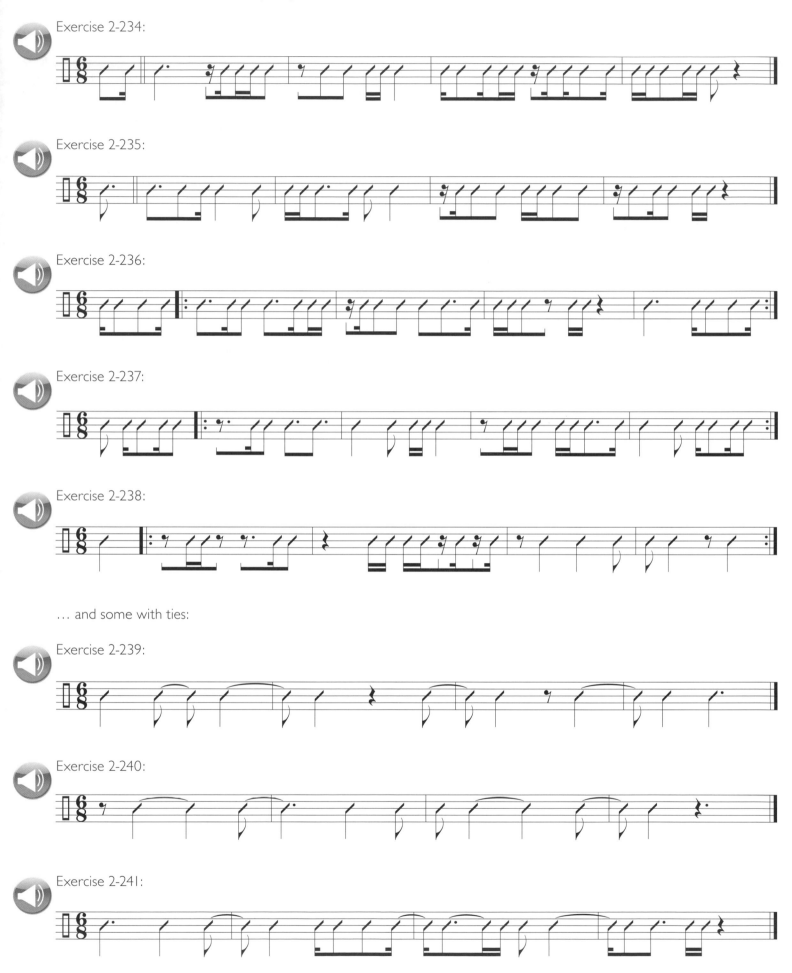

Exercise 2-242:

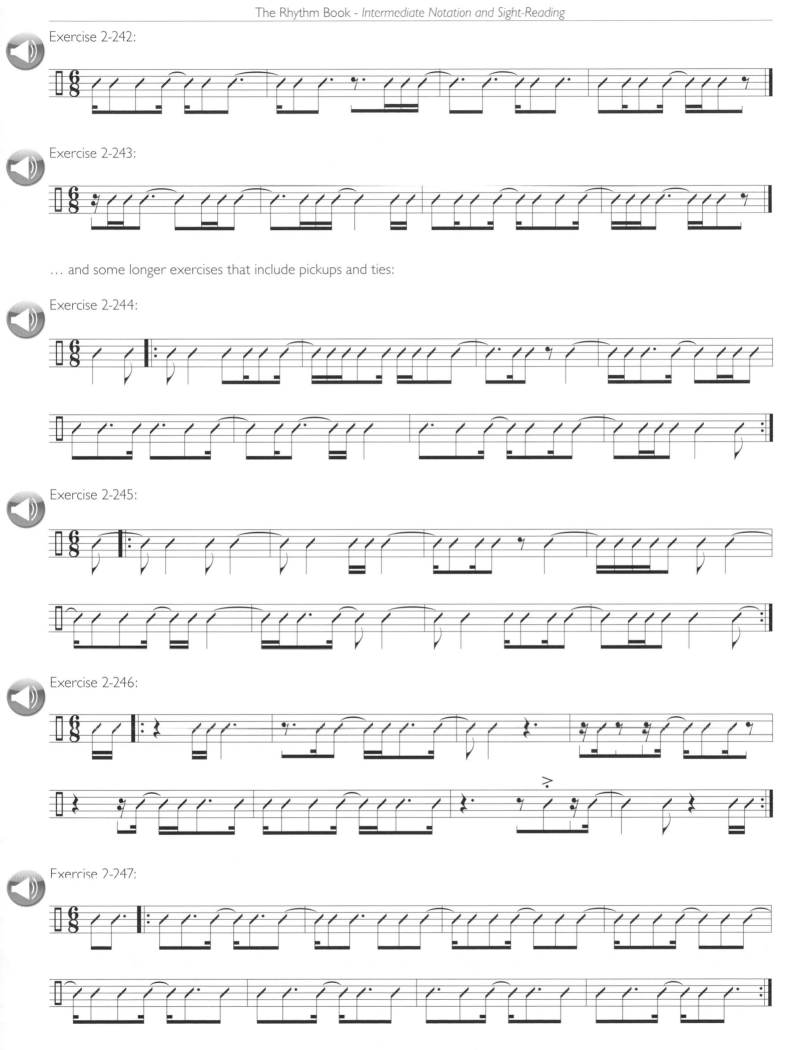

Exercise 2-243:

… and some longer exercises that include pickups and ties:

Exercise 2-244:

Exercise 2-245:

Exercise 2-246:

Exercise 2-247:

... and some with pitches:

Exercise 2-248:

Exercise 2-249:

Exercise 2-250:

Exercise 2-251:

... and some multi-part exercises:

Exercise 2-252:

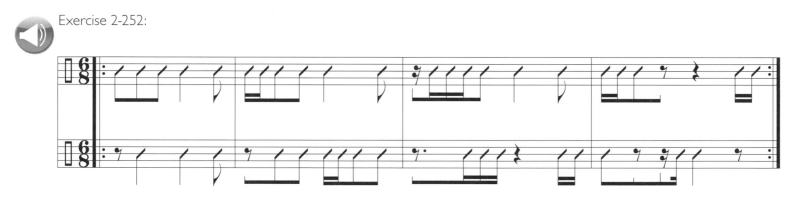

Exercise 2-253:

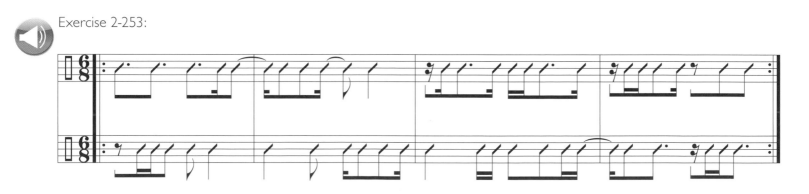

Exercise 2-254:

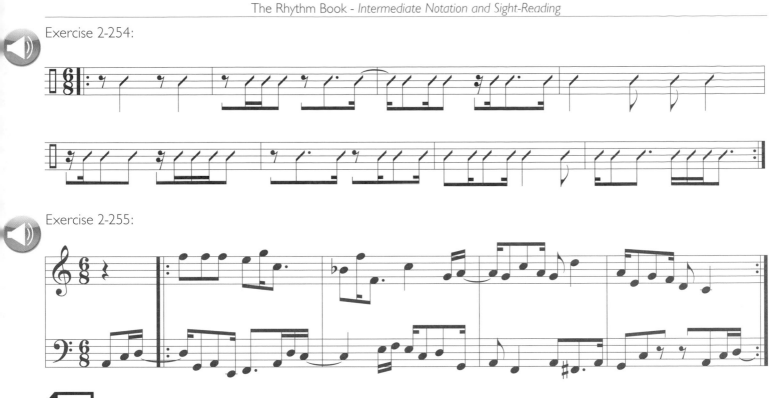

Exercise 2-255:

Transcribe 6/8 examples with ties and pickups, using Worksheet 2-W-043. Transcribe 6/8 multipart examples using Worksheet 2-W-044.

Avoiding a Common Mistake: Triplet 8ths in Triple Meter

Perhaps the most common notation problem I see from people inexperienced in writing triple meters is that they put triplet signs over groups of eighth notes when, in fact, there are no triplets:

Example 2-164:

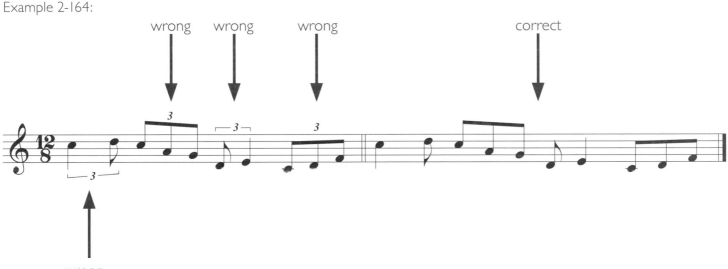

Triplet eighth notes in a triple meter are very unusual. In the following example, the first three triplet eighth notes would happen in the time normally taken by two eighth notes—so, there is still another eighth note left in order to fill the first dotted quarter.

Example 2-165:

In order to play this example accurately, you must make sure that you feel the duration of the first quarter note in the beginning of the first dotted quarter:

Example 2-166:

… and then divide it into three equal parts:

Example 2-167:

Be careful to feel that the fourth note in the example falls right on the third eighth note within the first dotted quarter:

Example 2-168:

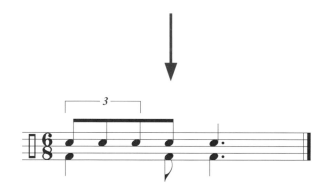

A common mistake is to actually sing what's written in the first bar of the following example, when you intend to sing the triplet eighth note figure (shown in the third bar). Since we have not yet worked on "4 in the time of 3," in the second bar, I have written something identical to the first bar but without using "4:3." As you can see, if you correctly sing the third bar, your fourth note falls right on the third eighth note in the bar; if you make the common mistake I've shown, you are singing the fourth note later:

Example 2-169:

Because I want you to see how difficult and unusual triplet-eighth notes are in a triple meter context, I showed the above example. However, this was largely so that you remember NOT to put triplet signs over regular eighth notes in a triple meter context (unless it is actually this unusual kind of rhythm you want)!

12/8 Feels

Although our focus for now is solely on how to write and read in triple meters, you should be aware that you may be doing this in the context of a few different feels written in 12/8. A common one has at its core this kind of Afro-Cuban feel:

Example 2-170:

Another common 12/8 feel is one associated with "doo-wop" of the 1950s and early 1960s, and also with some gospel music:

Example 2-171:

Other less common 12/8 feels will be discussed further in THE RHYTHM BOOK—*Odd Meters and Changing Meters*, but an interesting one to check out is in the piece "Mademoiselle Mabry" on the Miles Davis recording *Filles De Kilimanjaro* (here is the first bar):

Example 2-172:

12/8 Exercises

Here are some exercises in 12/8, including some with ties, pickups, pitches, and multiple parts:

Exercise 2-256:

Exercise 2-257:

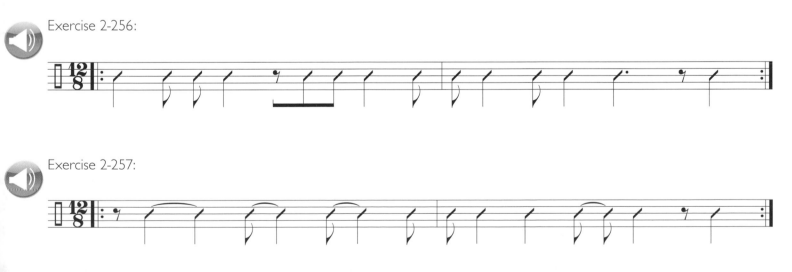

117

Exercise 2-258:

Exercise 2-259:

Exercise 2-260:

Exercise 2-261:

Exercise 2-262:

Exercise 2-263:

Exercise 2-264:

Exercise 2-265:

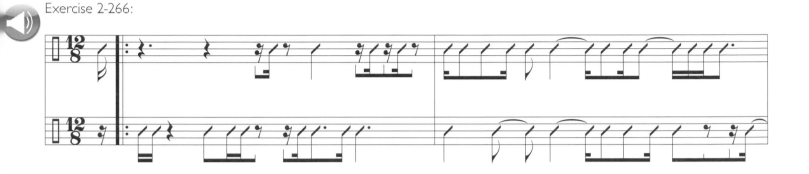

Exercise 2-266:

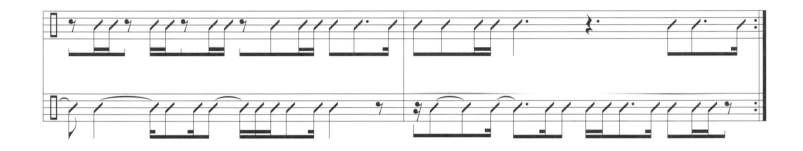

Exercise 2-267:

Transcribe 12/8 examples using Worksheet 2-W-045 and Worksheet 2-W-046.

9/8 Exercises
Like 6/8 and 12/8, we feel 9/8 grouped by dotted quarter (in the case of 9/8, three of them). Here are exercises to practice sight-reading in 9/8:

Exercise 2-268:

Exercise 2-269:

Exercise 2-270:

Exercise 2-271:

Exercise 2-272:

Exercise 2-273:

Exercise 2-274:

Exercise 2-275:

Exercise 2-276:

Transcribe 9/8 examples using Worksheet 2-W-047.

Other Triple Meters

Other triple meters work just like 6/8, 9/8, and 12/8. We feel the music in dotted quarters, and group things that way when we notate in these meters.

When we looked at the possible figures that can happen per dotted quarter, we already got an extensive review of 3/8, so we will not give more 3/8 examples here. But we will look at examples in some other triple meters.

In 15/8 (which feels like five dotted quarters per bar):

Exercise 2-277:

Exercise 2-278:

Exercise 2-279:

Exercise 2-280:

Exercise 2-281:

Exercise 2-282:

In 18/8 (it feels like six dotted quarters per bar):

Exercise 2-283:

Exercise 2-284:

Exercise 2-285:

Exercise 2-286:

In 21/8 (it feels like seven dotted quarters per bar):

Exercise 2-287:

Exercise 2-288:

Exercise 2-289:

Exercise 2-290:

All of the above examples in other triple meters have been well-notated; as recommended, the music is grouped and beamed to show the required beats, which are dotted quarters.

Transcribe examples in these other triple meters using and Worksheet 2-W-048 and Worksheet 2-W-049.

Correcting Poorly Notated Triple Meters

We can reinforce our good habits in triple meter by practicing the correction of poorly notated examples. We previously corrected a few simple poorly notated 6/8 examples. Now, let us consider in more detail the process of correcting poorly notated triple meters.

If faced with examples that fail to show required dotted quarters, such as this:

Example 2-173:

... we first think of how the rhythm falls by dotted quarter (this intermediate step can be done in your head if you can do so without writing it):

Example 2-174:

... and then simplify to produce this well-notated version:

Example 2-175:

Similarly, this example fails to show required dotted quarters:

Example 2-176:

... so we do this intermediate step, either on paper or in our heads:

Example 2-177:

... and simplify to this well-notated version:

Example 2-178:

We cannot beam quarter notes. Sometimes, at the 16th level, when a note within the dotted quarter lasts at least four 16ths and could be written as a quarter note, people find it so visually appealing to have every dotted quarter beamed, that they will intentionally show some unrequired beats in order to do so. Here are a couple examples of rewriting the previous example in this way:

Example 2-179:

Example 2-180:

> Personally, I somewhat prefer the last version. Yet I would not necessarily advocate showing unrequired beats even in this example; the choice is yours. What do you think? Is one of the variations in the above example easier for you to read than the others? You can use the one you prefer.

With another example that fails to show each dotted quarter:

Example 2-181:

… try simplifying it without writing down the intermediate step. You should produce this version:

Example 2-182:

If we see an example that shows unrequired beats unnecessarily (as did our intermediate steps), such as this:

Example 2-183:

… we simplify it to this:

Example 2-184:

If an example is not beamed correctly, with many unbeamed "orphan" notes that belong to the same dotted quarter note, as in this example:

Example 2-185:

… we beam the notes to show the dotted quarters:

Example 2-186:

Again, unbeamed notes that should be beamed by the pulse:

Example 2-187:

… should be beamed correctly:

Example 2-188:

Here, unbeamed notes also are written so that they do not show required beats:

Example 2-189:

… write the intermediate step if it helps:

Example 2-190:

… and simplify to produce a well-notated example:

Example 2-191:

Similarly, correct this:

Example 2-192:

… so that it is written like this:

Example 2-193:

Here, instead of leaving unbeamed "orphan" notes that share a beam, the writer has mistakenly beamed notes across the dotted quarters:

Example 2-194:

Correct it by beaming only the notes that belong to the dotted quarters:

Example 2-195:

 Practice correcting poorly notated triple meter examples using Worksheet 2-W-050 and Worksheet 2-W-051.

32nd Note Triple Meter Notation

Although triple meter music is usually at the eighth-note or 16th-note levels, let's consider triple meter music at the 32nd-note level. The notation should beam by dotted quarter (with secondary beams) but, within each dotted quarter, beam the notes that are part of each eighth note. Here is an example of well-notated 32nd note triple meter music that does this correctly:

Example 2-196:

When we sight-read such an example, we feel the dotted quarter as the "big pulse" but, within that, also feel each eighth note:

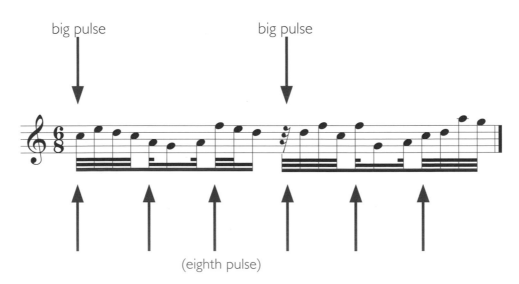

Meters with Two, Four, and Eight Beats

In *THE RHYTHM BOOK—Notation and Sight-Reading: Quarter Notes, Eighth Notes, and Triplet Eighth Notes*, we saw that, in 4/4, the quarter note is felt as the pulse. We also briefly looked at 2/4, another meter in which the quarter note is felt as the pulse. In this volume, we examined 3/4, in which the quarter note is felt as the pulse.

But there are meters in which something other than the quarter note is felt as the pulse; the way the time signature is written tells us what note to feel as the pulse. The bottom number (denominator) in the time signature indicates the duration of a "beat" in the meter. If it is "4," the beat felt is the quarter note; if it is "2," the beat felt is a half note; if it is "8," it is an eighth note; if "16," it is a 16th note.

> We have already explored a group of meters in which the quarter note is not felt as the pulse, but they are quite exceptional. In triple meters, although the bottom number (denominator) in the time signature is "8" and we can feel the eighth notes in these meters, it is dotted quarter notes that we feel as the primary pulse. These are exceptional because, with all the other meters we encounter, the primary pulse is defined solely by the note indicated by the denominator.

Therefore, if we choose the correct tempo for each, the following exercises not only sound the same but also feel the same. In each of these examples, the stem-down notes show the pulse that is felt, and the stem-up notes show the rhythm.

Example 2-197:

We feel the half notes as the pulse in this example in 4/2:

Example 2-198:

... and the eighth notes as the pulse in 4/8:

Example 2-199:

... and the 16th notes as the pulse in 4/16:

Example 2-200:

Notice that our example in 4/8 could have been written in 2/4 and would look the same:
Example 2-201:

… but, in 2/4, we would feel the quarter notes as the beat, where in 4/8 we feel the eighth notes as the beat.
The required beats to show in each meter follow from what we would expect. With quarter note music in 4/4, the only required beat to show was "1." That means that, at the quarter level, we must show each whole note of music. Similarly, in 4/2 at the quarter level, we must show each whole note of music, but there are two of these per bar, so we show the first beat of each."

2/2 or **cut time** ("alla breve" in classical music), discussed previously and often represented by the ¢, is perhaps the most common meter in which the denominator is not "4."

In contexts related to jazz and contemporary music, you will often see music written in cut time that has a samba feel (or, sometimes, a calypso feel). For example:

Example 2-202:

Interestingly, this is almost entirely an American interpretation of samba (so it is how you might see a samba notated by a fusion band, or by Chick Corea).

Brazilian musicians will almost always write genuine sambas in 2/4, with rhythms at the 16th-note level. So, a Brazilian composer writing the same rhythm we saw in the previous example would usually notate it:

Example 2-203:

> In the interest of space, I have included only a limited number of cut time examples throughout the books. However, it is important to be comfortable with cut time. You can easily practice many examples by sight-reading the many eighth note examples in THE RHYTHM BOOK—Beginning Notation and Sight-Reading as though they were written in cut time.

For one more look at writing the same rhythm in different ways based on what we choose as the pulse, consider these examples which have eight beats per measure.

In 8/4:

Example 2-204:

In 8/8:

Example 2-205:

In 8/16:

Example 2-206:

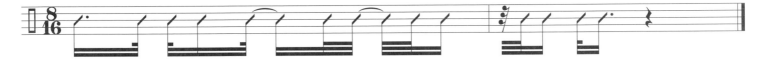

Again, notice that the same rhythms could have been written but would have felt different if the meters had been named differently. For instance, Example 2-204 could have been written in 4/2, but would have been felt with four beats, not eight:

Example 2-207:

> Some of the meters we're examining here are ones we seldom see in a jazz and contemporary music context. 4/2, for example, is seen mainly in older classical music, e.g. pieces from the early 17th century (G. Frescobaldi's "Aria Con Variazioni"), and the 1860s (some sections of the "German Requiem" by Brahms) but rarely in music written today. Bach even wrote a piece in 2/1 (the Gigue in his Partita No. 6). Although these meters are used infrequently, it is important to understand how the denominator expresses the pulse. This will serve as a foundation for odd meters, discussed in the next section.

Here are some exercises in these meters. In the first of each, I explicitly remind you of the pulse to feel (shown stem-down):

In 4/2:

Exercise 2-291:

Exercise 2-292:

Exercise 2-293:

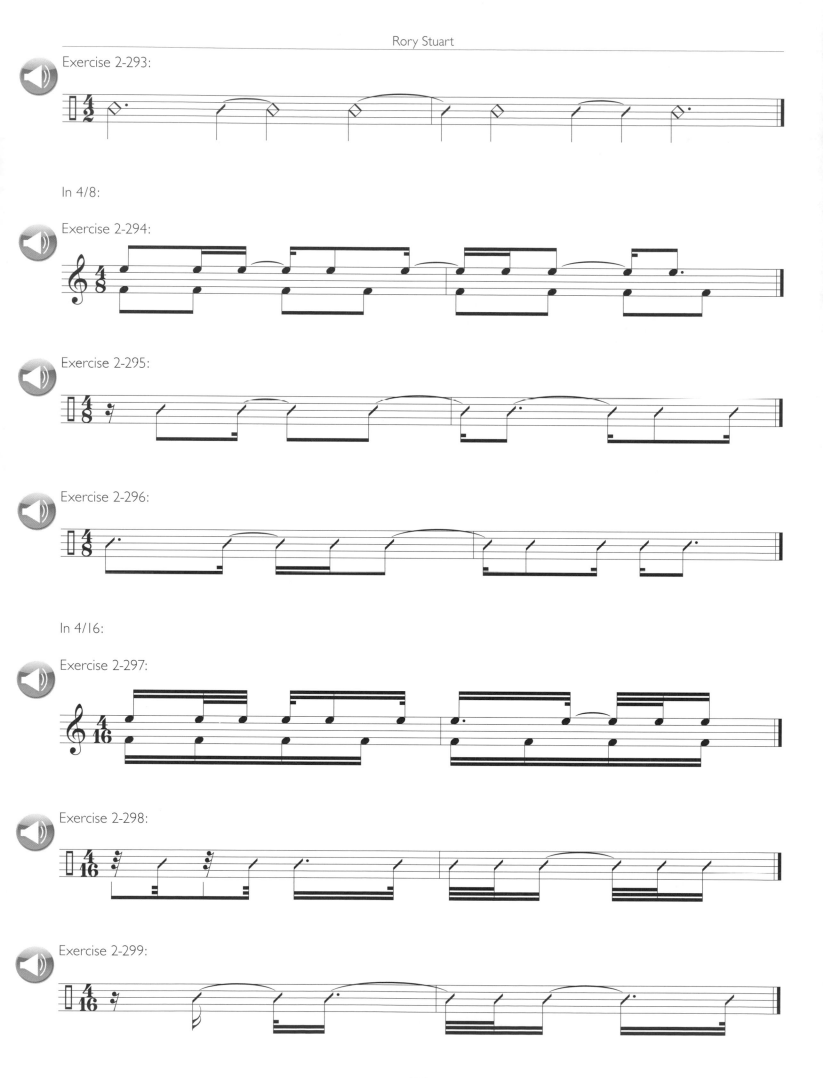

In 4/8:

Exercise 2-294:

Exercise 2-295:

Exercise 2-296:

In 4/16:

Exercise 2-297:

Exercise 2-298:

Exercise 2-299:

We can practice converting from a rhythm written in one of these meters to a rhythm that that sounds the same in another meter. For instance:

Exercise 2-300:

… and:

Exercise 2-301:

For another example:

Exercise 2-302:

… and:

Exercise 2-303:

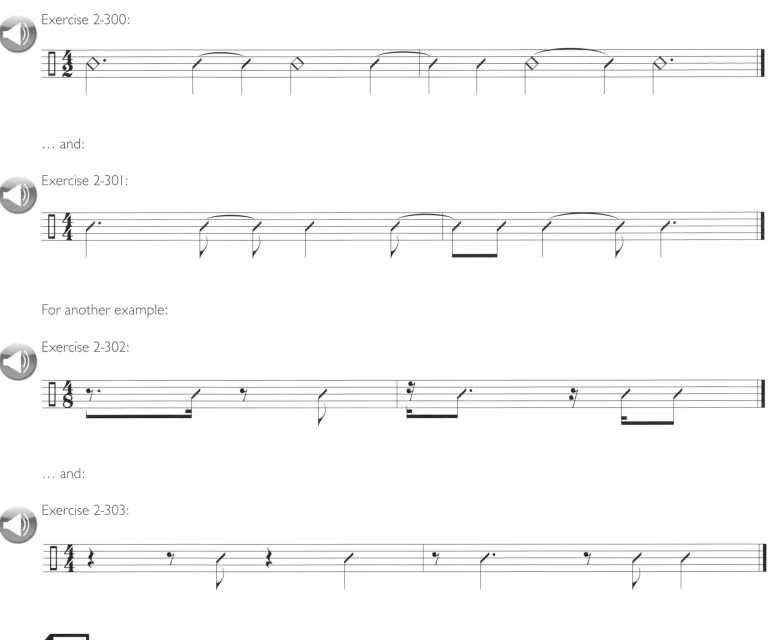

 Practice converting between duple meters using Worksheet 2-W-052.

Odd Meters

We have looked at notation so far for 4/4 and 3/4, for duple meters such as 2/4, 2/2, 4/2, and 4/8, and for triple meters, such as 6/8, 9/8, and 12/8. Now we will consider other meters.

> These other meters are often called "odd" meters. To be clear, we say "odd" not in the sense of "strange" but in the sense of an "odd number." However, even this is not quite right; an odd number is one that is not divisible by 2, but 14/4 would commonly be called an "odd meter" even though 14 is divisible by 2. In common usage, the expression "odd meter" is used to mean "meters that are not 4/4, 2/4, or cut time." Of these, our discussion here addresses those that are not triple meters.

"Odd meters" such as 5/4 and 7/4, are written to group the notes by the division felt for the meter. In *THE RHYTHM BOOK—Odd Meters and Changing Meters*, we have an in-depth examination of performing these odd meters; for now, we are only concerned that you understand how to notate them. Here is an example in 5/4 using the most common division of that meter into a 3/4 plus a 2/4 (so we make certain to write the measure as it would be if it were a well-notated bar of 3/4 followed by a well-notated bar of 2/4):

Example 2-208:

It is really only at the eighth-note level and above where we need to concern ourselves with those divisions; once we get to the 16th-note level, we just show rhythms beat by beat:

Example 2-209:

Like 5/4, the same 3+2 division applies to 5/8, except it is divided into 3/8 plus 2/8. Here we see an example at the eighth-note level:

Example 2-210:

… and here is an example at 16th-note level:

Example 2-211:

The same idea applies to other odd meters: we need to know how the meter is felt, then divide it accordingly. To take one more example, the most common 7/4 is felt as 4/4 plus 3/4, so one measure of it should look like a well-notated bar of 4/4 followed by a well-notated bar of 3/4:

Example 2-212:

You may also see a notation form described as "composite meters," in which a single measure is written as though it contained a series of two or more meters; this is a way to show how the time is broken up. Béla Bartók used these frequently. Here, in the middle bar, is an example that you will in find in music such as "Here Comes the Sun" by the Beatles:

Example 2-213:

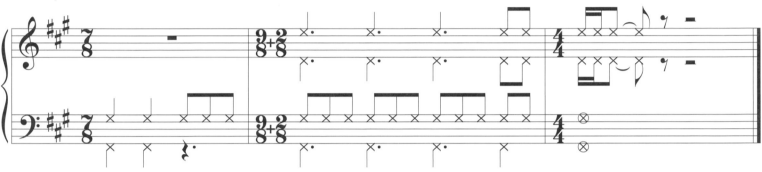

Now you know what you need to in order to correctly notate odd meters. For the exciting and much deeper discussion of how to play them, please see *THE RHYTHM BOOK—Odd Meters and Changing Meters.*

How to Show a Meter Change
To show a change from one meter to another, we put the new time signature at the start of the measure:

Example 2-214:

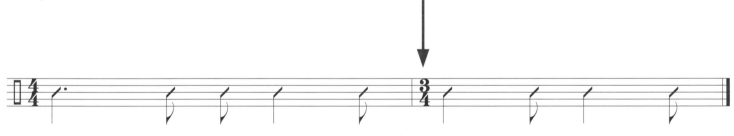

If the change happens as we go from one line on the page to the next, we may also show a "courtesy" time signature at the end of the previous line.

Example 2-215:

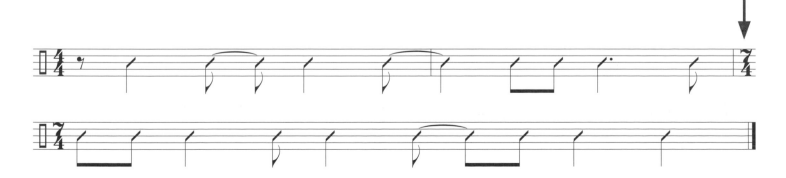

Combining Rhythmic Figures at Different Rates in Other Meters

There is nothing conceptually different between combining rhythmic figures at different rates in non-4/4 meters and doing so in 4/4; in each case, we can adjust the internal grid we feel as the rate changes. Nevertheless, we can look at some examples to improve our familiarity with this.

Here is an example in 3/4 that changes from eighth-note level to 16th-note level:

Example 2-216:

Here we change in 3/4 from 16th-note level to quarter-note level:

Example 2-217:

In this example, the meter changes from 3/4 to 4/4, and we change from triplet-eighth level to 16th level:

Example 2-218:

Here, with the same meter change, the rate of the notes change from eighth-note triplets to 16th-note triplets:

Example 2-219:

Here we change from eighth-note level in 3/4 to 16th-note level in 4/8.

Example 2-220:

Notice in the previous example that, while you feel a change in the rate of pulse when you go to 4/8, the written rhythms themselves would sound the same if you went to 2/4:

Example 2-221:

Here, we stay in 5/4, but the rate of notes changes from eighth notes to 16ths. Play it with the repeat to help you hear the meter and become accustomed to the change in rate of notes:

Example 2-222:

Here we change from 4/4 to 3/4 with the rate of notes at triplet-16th level; then, within the 3/4, the rate changes to 16th-note level:

Example 2-223:

Finally, here we are in 3/4 and, within that meter, change from quarter-note level to 16th level; then, the meter changes to 5/4 and, after a bar at 16th-note level, we change to triplet-eighth-note level:

Example 2-224:

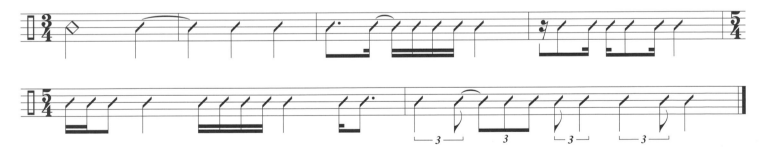

 Practice transcribing examples in which the rate of notes changes, using Worksheet 2-W-053.

Rhythmic Isoforms: Different Ways of Writing Rhythms That Sound the Same

We have already seen that rhythms that sound the same can be written in different ways – for example, see Example 2-197 on page 129 through Example 2-201 on page 130, and Examples 2-202 and 2-203 on page 130.

I call these "rhythmic isoforms:" different ways of representing a rhythm on the written page which will sound identical to a listener (who does not know the underlying meter or the pulse being felt). Review of rhythmic isoforms is a good way to reinforce your understanding of rhythmic notation. Here are some examples.

2/4 and Cut Time

As we have noted already in Example 2-202 and Example 2-203, rhythms in 2/4 and cut time can sound identical. Here is another example of rhythms in these meters that sound identical:

Example 2-225:

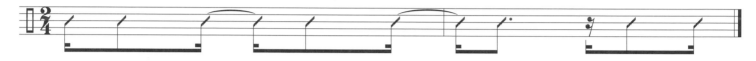

Example 2-226:

2/4 and 4/4

Here are some rhythmic isoforms in 2/4 and 4/4:

Example 2-227:

Example 2-228:

Similarly:

Example 2-229:

Example 2-230:

4/4 and 4/2

As we saw previously, we can have rhythmic isoforms in 4/4 and 4/2. Here are more examples:

Example 2-231:

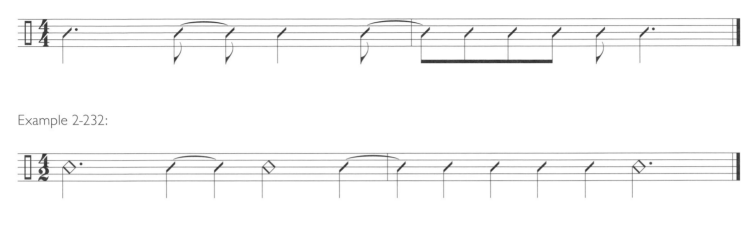

Example 2-232:

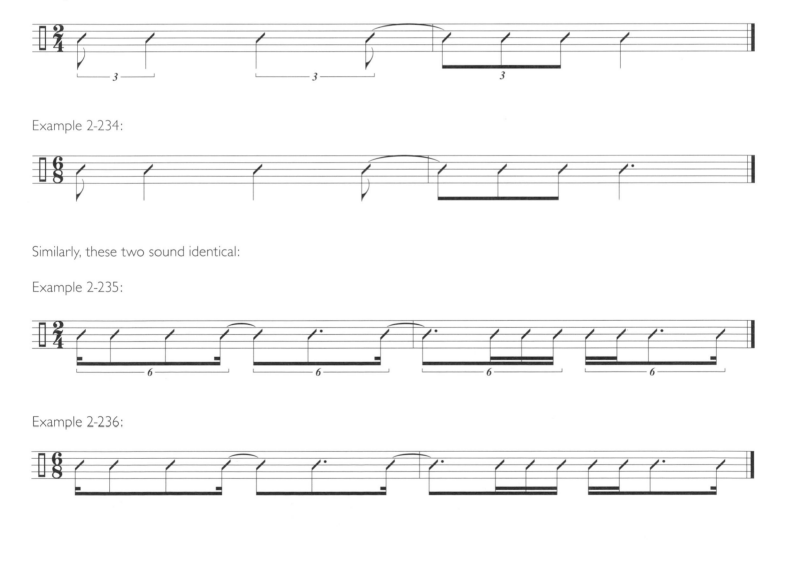

2/4 and 6/8

By making the quarter note in 2/4 and the dotted quarter in 6/8 equal, we can create rhythmic isoforms between these meters. The following two examples sound identical if played at tempos where the quarter note in 2/4 takes as long as does the dotted quarter note in 6/8:

Example 2-233:

Example 2-234:

Similarly, these two sound identical:

Example 2-235:

Example 2-236:

4/4 and 12/8

As with the relationship between the previous examples in 2/4 and 6/8, rhythms in 4/4 and 12/8 can sound identical if the quarter note figures in 4/4 are made to sound the same as the dotted quarter figures in 12/8. These examples sound identical:

Example 2-237:

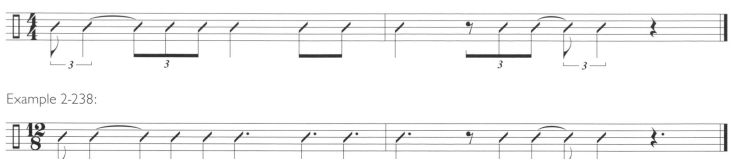

Example 2-238:

... as do these:

Example 2-239:

Example 2-240:

2/4 and 12/8

Although less obvious, we can make examples in 2/4 and 12/8 sound identical if the figures in each quarter note of 2/4 sound the same as those in each dotted half note of 12/8. Here is a rhythm that sounds the same in these meters:

Example 2-241:

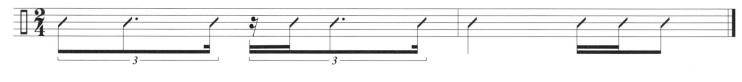

Example 2-242:

... and here is another:

Example 2-243:

Example 2-244:

3/4 and 6/8

A measure of 3/4 and one of 6/8 do not sound the same because of the different way the pulse is felt and the music is accented. But, we can write two bars of fast 3/4 that sound the same as a slower bar of 6/8:

Example 2-245:

Example 2-246:

For another example:

Example 2-247:

Example 2-248:

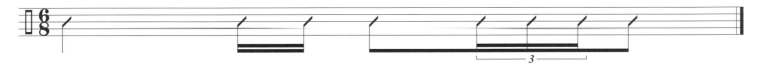

Similarly, we could write four bars of fast 3/4 and a rhythm that sounds the same notated in one slower bar of 12/8:

Example 2-249:

Example 2-250:

4/4 with Triplet 16ths and Fast 3/4

For another example that is not obvious, a rhythm written in a measure of 4/4, especially if it has triplet-16th notes, can sound the same as a rhythm written in 4 bars of 3/4 at a fast tempo, or 4 bars of 6/8 at a fast tempo.

Here is a rhythm written in 4/4:

Example 2-251:

… and the same rhythm written in 4 bars of 3/4:

Example 2-252:

… and the same rhythm written in 2 bars of 6/8:

Example 2-253:

  Practice converting between isoforms using Worksheet 2-W-054.

Multiple Isoforms

Finally, we examine a rhythm written in several different isoforms. Played at the right tempos, each of these sound the same.

As four bars of 6/4:

Example 2-254:

As four bars of 3/4:

Example 2-255:

As four bars of 4/4:

Example 2-256:

As two bars of 6/8:

Example 2-257:

As one bar of 4/4:

Example 2-258:

As one bar of 4/2:

Example 2-259:

As two bars of 12/8:

Example 2-260:

As one bar of 2/4:

Example 2-261:

As one bar of 12/8:

Example 2-262:

As eight bars of 3/4:

Example 2-263:

In addition to the ten versions we have just considered, try to create some more versions of your own with this rhythm.

 Practice converting another example rhythm into isoforms using Worksheet 2-W-055.

 Based on the examples we have looked at, create your own rhythm example and think of and write it in as many isoforms as you can, using Worksheet 2-W-056.

Why Choose One Notation Over Another?
With so many possible ways to notate a rhythm, how do we make the choice of which to use?

In general, there are three criteria:

1) What feel is desired in the rhythm section? A rhythm section will typically play much differently performing four bars of 3/4 (as in Example 2-255) than they will performing one bar of 2/4 (as in Example 2-261) or four bars of 6/4 (as in Example 2-254). Think of the rhythm feel you want from the rhythm section and choose the appropriate meter. This is often the most important criteria. While it is possible to put notes in the parts that say things such as "make this bar of 4/4 feel like two bars of fast 12/8," these can often be confusing and slow up rehearsal for thought and discussion by the performers. Writing in the meter that naturally produces the feel we want generally works best.

2) What is the context of the song? Consider in what meter and at what rate of pulse the other sections are written. What happens immediately before and after the section in question? Song form can have an influence—if it is a blues, we are often tempted to find a way to write it that takes 12 bars (rather than, for example, six bars).

3) In what notation is it easiest to read? Although the previous two criteria should take precedence, ease of reading should also be considered. It is clear, for example, that, among the previous examples, many people would find Example 2-261 more difficult to read than Example 2-255. Everything else being equal, you should choose what is easier to read.

Where to Go from Here

If you have mastered the materials in this book, you have a solid foundation in rhythmic notation and sight-reading. You can continue to practice to hone these abilities in order to get faster and more accurate, so they will feel effortless. While sight-reading and transcribing are just tools, they are very useful skills to have. There is much more to rhythm than writing or reading it from the page and, using the skills you've acquired, we can proceed to the next volumes of this series to focus on rhythmic concepts and practices that will enrich your performances, as well as any composition and arrangements that you do. *THE RHYTHM BOOK—Rhythmic Development and Performance in 4/4* has as its focus 4/4 styles including swing, funk, Afro-Cuban, Brazilian, ballads; relationship to the beat; soloist/rhythm section interaction; developing a rhythmic idea; and more. As its title indicates, the entire volume of *THE RHYTHM BOOK— Crossrhythms on 4/4* is devoted to the wonderfully fun and challenging topic of crossrhythms (also sometimes called polymeters or groupings). *THE RHYTHM BOOK—Odd Meters and Changing Meters* and *THE RHYTHM BOOK—Superimposition and Subdivision, Metric Modulation, Feel Modulation and Displacement* explore more advanced topics including odd meters, changing meters, metric modulation, feel modulation, rhythmic superimposition and subdivision, crossrhythms on odd meters, and more.

Appendices
Appendix I – A Musical Anecdote

Many years ago, I received a call from Brother Jack McDuff, a legendary organ player I had never met, but knew of due to the famous folks who had been in his band, including George Benson and Pat Martino. He asked me to join his band, which was playing in Gary, Indiana that night (I was in Boulder, Colorado), but I needed to get there in time for the first set THAT NIGHT! This was in the days before cell phones, internet, etc.—it took some quick thinking to figure out a way to do this. I raced to the airport in Denver, just barely caught the last plane to Chicago that would get me there on time, got a bus from Chicago to Gary, got to the hotel, raced upstairs to a room, changed clothes hurriedly, raced down to the club, plugged in my amp, plugged in my guitar as the band was ready to begin the first set, and Jack called out "49"—there was a large binder with numbered charts on a music stand in front of me, and I opened it to chart #49 just as Jack counted off the piece. The entire first set was like this: "32," "112," "17." As Jack would call charts, the saxophone player (Ramon Morris) and I would read them, as Jack and the drummer (Gerryck King) swung their butts off behind us. There's a lot more to the story that followed—actually the best parts of the story are things I can't write about in an instructional book, but ask me about them if we meet in person! For now, let me tell you what I saw when I opened up to the first chart.

Jack had written hip arrangements on largely bluesy tunes (with swing or funk feels), in which the saxophone and guitar both played lines, sometimes unison but often harmonized or even counter-lines. The charts were quite difficult to read – but, when you played them, you realized they were difficult largely because of how he had notated them, the actual things you were playing were not too difficult. I don't have copies of these charts anymore, but I'll give you an idea of the kind of things he would do in his notation (another example is Example 2-047 on page 23):

Example 2-264:

Before I comment on the rhythmic aspect let me mention, in passing, the issue with accidentals. He would write a piece in a key signature, then add accidentals. His choice of whether to spell something with a sharp sign or flat sign (e.g. G♯ or A♭) seemed to be random, and had nothing to do with the key signature or the harmonic function of the note or how it related to the chord it was played on. Later in the measure, after there had been a mix of sharps and flats earlier on, you had to remember with each pitch you saw (no courtesy accidentals!) what previous accidentals applied to it. As you can see in the above example, this was no easy task—in this example, in the first measure you have to remember through the measure that C and G are sharped, while the B and E stay flatted due to the key signature; in the second measure, you must remember that D is flatted and G is sharped. That will keep you on your toes when you are sight-reading music you've never seen or heard before, huh?

In terms of the rhythmic notation he used, he did show each note with its correct duration, and there were the correct number of beats in most measures. However, he wrote rhythms so that he rarely showed the "required beats" (he did not necessarily show any beats in the measure after "1"!) and it was very difficult to see any patterns; if you ever made a mistake, it was almost impossible to get back on track until the next measure.

Before we performed the next day, I looked through charts, lightly penciling in courtesy accidentals and rewrites of rhythms to make them more readable where there was too much for me to remember. Look at how much easier the above example was once it was better notated:

Example 2-265:

Why do you think Jack notated things the way he did? When I thought about it, I had a good idea of why he did this. Can you come up with an explanation? I think an essential clue, which you may not know unless you know his musical background, is that he spent nearly his entire career as a leader, playing charts that he himself wrote.

Appendix II – Practice Suggestions

In *THE RHYTHM BOOK—Beginning Notation and Sight-Reading*, I offered some suggestions about practice, including practicing with recordings, practicing with others, and ways to make rhythm more "physical." I won't replicate all those ideas here but, for your convenience, here is a table with some possible combinations you can use for voice, hands, and feet:

Voice	Hands	Feet
say "1 2 3 4"	clap or tap rhythm	(none)
say "1 2 3 4"	clap or tap rhythm	walk quarter notes
say "1 2 3 4"	clap or tap rhythm	tap "1"
say "1 2 3 4"	clap or tap rhythm	tap "1" and "3"
say "1 2 3 4"	clap or tap rhythm	tap "2" and "4"
(none)	clap or tap rhythm	walk quarter notes
(none)	clap or tap rhythm	tap "1"
(none)	clap or tap rhythm	tap "1" and "3"
(none)	clap or tap rhythm	tap "2" and "4"
sing rhythm	clap or tap quarter notes	(none)
sing rhythm	clap or tap "1"	(none)
sing rhythm	clap or tap "1" and "3"	(none)
sing rhythm	clap or tap "2" and "4"	(none)
sing rhythm	clap or tap "3"	(none)
sing rhythm	clap or tap "1"	walk quarter notes
sing rhythm	clap or tap "1" and "3"	walk quarter notes
sing rhythm	clap or tap "2" and "4"	walk quarter notes
sing rhythm	clap or tap "3"	walk quarter notes
sing rhythm	clap or tap "1"	tap quarter notes
sing rhythm	clap or tap "1"	tap "1" and "3"
sing rhythm	clap or tap "1"	tap "2" and "4"
sing rhythm	clap or tap "2"	tap "1"
sing rhythm	clap or tap "3"	tap "1"
sing rhythm	clap or tap "1"	tap "3"
sing rhythm	clap or tap "1"	tap "2" and "4"
sing rhythm	snap fingers on quarter notes	(none)
sing rhythm	snap fingers on "1"	(none)
sing rhythm	snap fingers on "1" and "3"	(none)
sing rhythm	snap fingers on "2" and "4"	(none)
sing rhythm	snap fingers on "3"	(none)
sing rhythm	snap fingers on "1"	walk quarter notes
sing rhythm	snap fingers on "1" and "3"	walk quarter notes
sing rhythm	snap fingers on "2" and "4"	walk quarter notes
sing rhythm	snap fingers on "3"	walk quarter notes
sing rhythm	snap fingers on "1"	tap quarter notes
sing rhythm	snap fingers on "1"	tap "1" and "3"
sing rhythm	snap fingers on "1"	tap "2" and "4"
sing rhythm	snap fingers on "2"	tap "1"
sing rhythm	snap fingers on "3"	tap "1"
sing rhythm	snap fingers on "1"	tap "3"
sing rhythm	snap fingers on "1"	tap "2" and "4"

Voice	Left Hand	Right Hand	Left Foot	Right Foot
(none)	tap "2" and "4"	tap rhythm	tap "1"	(none)
(none)	snap "2" and "4"	tap rhythm	(none)	tap "1"
(none)	tap rhythm	tap "2" and "4"	tap "1"	(none)
(none)	tap rhythm	tap "1" and "3"	(none)	(none)
sing rhythm	tap "2" and "4"	tap "1"	(none)	(none)
sing rhythm	tap "2" and "4"	(none)	(none)	tap "1"
sing rhythm	snap "1"	(none)	tap "2" and "4"	tap "1" and "3"

It is not important to practice all of the variations in this table, but it is useful to try some of them and practice any that are not immediately easy. Also, make up variations of your own!

Appendix III – Exercises for Piano and for Drums

Once you can sing and tap the rhythms in this book's exercises, you can practice them on your instrument. As spelled out in the appendices of *THE RHYTHM BOOK—Beginning Notation and Sight-Reading*, there are a number of approaches that can be used by pianists and drummers. Here are a few examples, using the more advanced material from this book.

For piano, here is a 16th-note exercise without pitches:

Exercise 2-304:

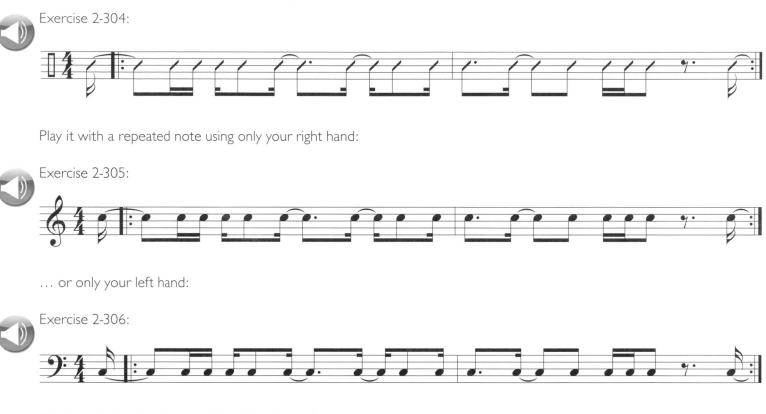

Play it with a repeated note using only your right hand:

Exercise 2-305:

... or only your left hand:

Exercise 2-306:

Play it in rhythmic unison with both hands on the same note:

Exercise 2-307:

... or in rhythmic unison on different notes:

Exercise 2-308:

Play it with one hand, while playing on beat one with the other hand:

Exercise 2-309:

Exercise 2-310:

… or a different beat of your choosing:

Exercise 2-311:

Exercise 2-312:

… or on beats one and three:

Exercise 2-313:

Exercise 2-314:

… or on beats two and four:

Exercise 2-315:

Exercise 2-316:

You can choose pitches for an exercise such as this, for example:

Exercise 2-317:

Again, do the things we just did, but using these pitches:

Exercise 2-318:

Exercise 2-319:

Exercise 2-320:

Exercise 2-321:

… and so forth.

Here are some of these ideas applied to a triplet 16th rhythm.

Choose a rhythm:

Exercise 2-322:

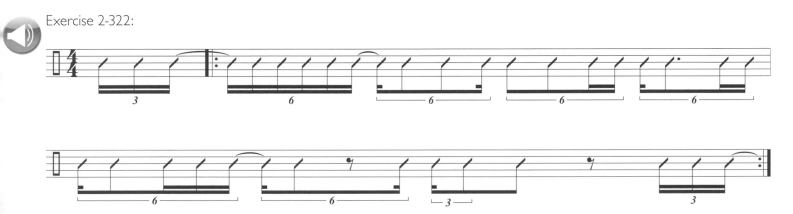

Play with a repeated note:

Exercise 2-323:

Add a part in the other hand:

Exercise 2-324:

Switch which hand plays the rhythm:

Exercise 2-325:

Choose pitches to play on the rhythm:

Exercise 2-326:

Play the rhythm with pitches using both hands in octaves:

Exercise 2-327:

Play the rhythm in one hand with something else in the other hand:

Exercise 2-328:

Switch which hand plays the rhythm:

Exercise 2-329:

We can also do these with triple meters, odd meters, rhythmic superimpositions, and metric modulations, but a full description of how to practice these is too lengthy for this appendix, and is provided in other volumes of *The Rhythm Book*.

Similarly, drummers can take a rhythm:

Exercise 2-330:

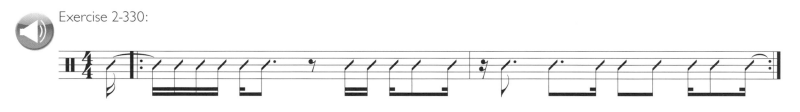

… and play it with one limb, while playing repeating parts with other limbs, such as:

Exercise 2-331:

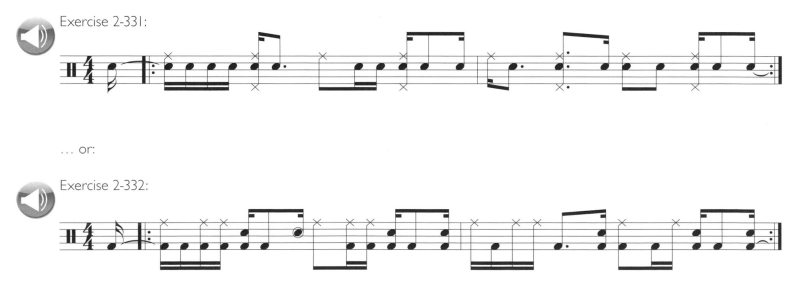

… or:

Exercise 2-332:

A drummer can also choose ways to distribute the rhythm between the limbs, such as:

Exercise 2-333:

… or:

Exercise 2-334:

Of course, you can add repeating parts with other limbs while distributing the rhythm between some limbs. If we add cymbal and hi-hat to Exercise 2-333, we might play:

Exercise 2-335:

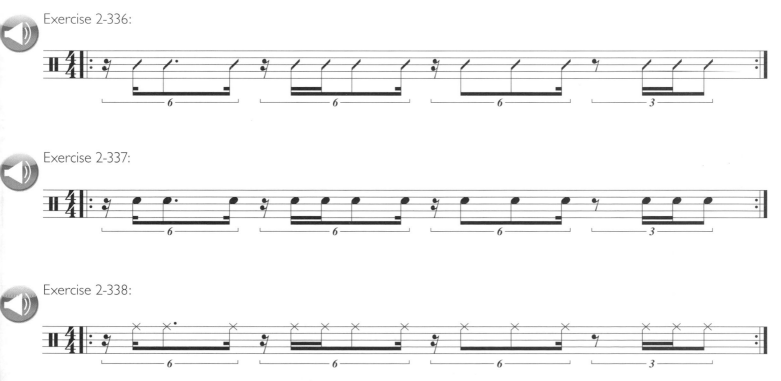

Here, we do similar things with a triplet-16th rhythm:

Exercise 2-336:

Exercise 2-337:

Exercise 2-338:

Exercise 2-339:

Exercise 2-340:

Exercise 2-341:

Exercise 2-342:

Exercise 2-343:

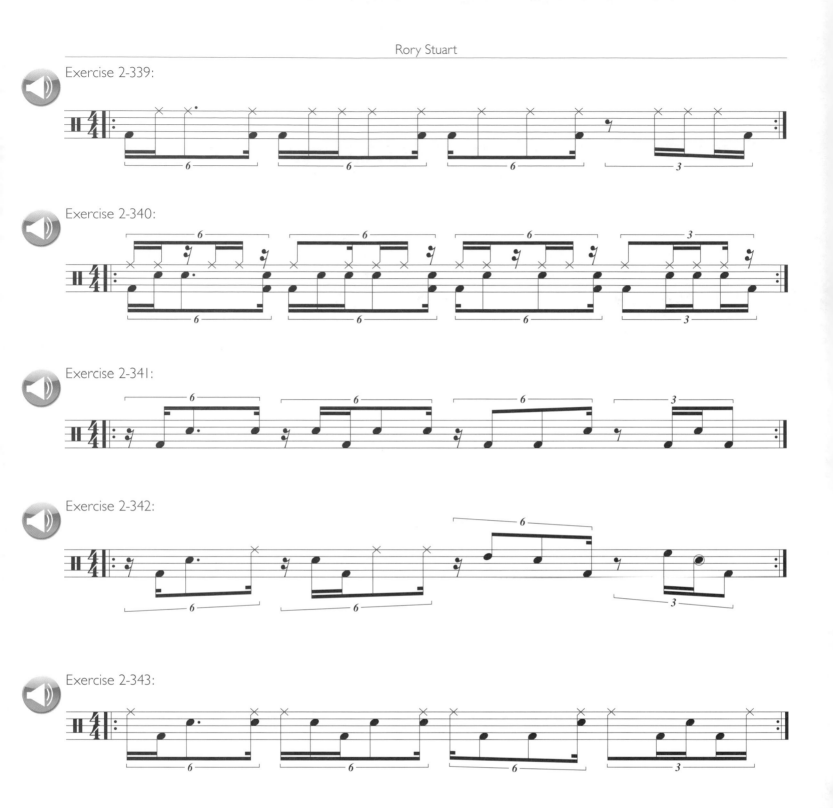

Appendix IV – "Road Map" Language

One always has the option of writing down a piece of music bar by bar from beginning to end. However, there are often some parts of the music that are repeated. There are symbols that allow us to show when sections are played multiple times; they give us a road map to navigate through a chart and write a chart more concisely.

Elements

Repeats

We have already introduced and used repeat signs. If we see repeat signs, we assume the passage is played a total of two times unless the chart says otherwise. If the passage should be played more than twice, it can be indicated:

Example 2-266:

To be clear, in the above example "3x" means that you should play the two bars that are between the repeat signs, then play them again, then play them a third time—so you will play a total of six bars.

Although very unconventional, one great idea in a case such as Example 2-266 is to put the "3x" above the bar just past the initial repeat sign, as well as at the end of the repeat. This immediately calls the reader's attention to the fact that this section will be repeated multiple times.

Another kind of repeat sign, the **one measure repeat** (or "one bar repeat") indicates to repeat only the bar that precedes it. So, a passage that we want to sound like this:

Example 2-267:

… could be written this way:

Example 2-268:

We can write multiple measure repeats if needed—we do not use a number (such as "3x") to indicate this with one measure repeats, we write them multiple times. So, for example, a passage we want to sound like this:

Example 2-269:

… could be written this way:

Example 2-270:

One measure repeats can also happen within a larger repeated section. So, if we wanted the entire previous example to be played twice, we could write it:

Example 2-271:

In exactly the same way that a one measure repeat sign indicates to repeat just the measure that precedes it, we can have **two measure repeat** signs, which indicate to repeat the two measures that precede—so this:

Example 2-272:

... could be written:

Example 2-273:

Repeats of even more measures in this style are possible, by writing a similar sign through more bars with the number of bars that are to be repeated written above it. I suggest you be careful not to overuse this style of repeats because it can add difficulty for the performers in remembering the passage to be repeated and keeping track of where they are in the music.

Multiple Endings
If the composer wants you to play a passage twice, but with a different last measure (or measures) the second time, a concise way to indicate this is to use **endings**. For example, to more concisely notate this:

Example 2-274:

... we could write it this way:

Example 2-275:

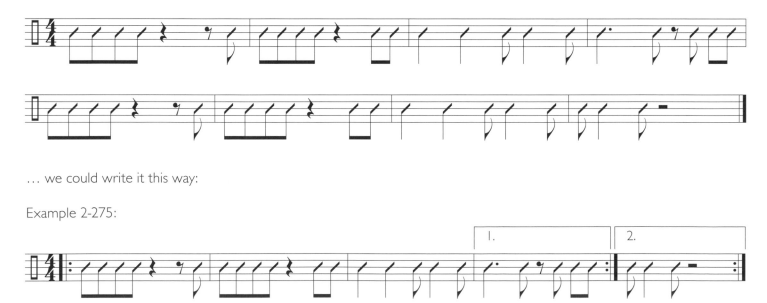

It is possible to have more endings – 1st ending, 2nd ending, 3rd ending, 4th ending, etc.
Example 2-276:

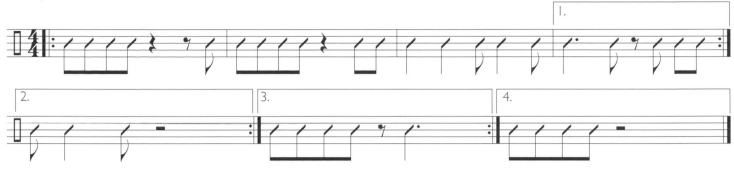

It is also possible, rather than writing out this:

Example 2-277:

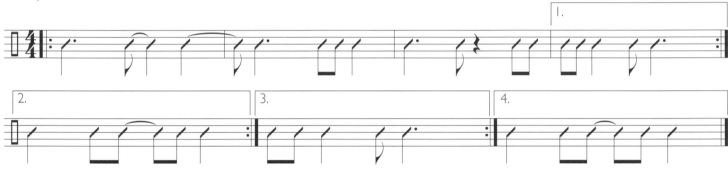

… to use multiple endings to indicate it this way:

Example 2-278:

Another possibility is to have an ending that repeats until a cue is given:

Example 2-279:

Note that, instead of "Last X," we could have written "On Cue."

D.C.

Capo literally means "head." **D.C.** (Da Capo) means "from the top" i.e. "from the beginning of the chart." Sometimes, especially in a chart when there are multiple sections with repeat signs, it can be a bit confusing to find the measure to which one returns. D.C. signs are always simple and clear, however; they indicate to go back and play from the very beginning of the chart.

Example 2-280:

The previous example does not, however, make full use of the D.C. sign. It would normally be combined with other instructions, e.g. "D.C. al Coda," which means "return and play from the very beginning of the chart, continue reading from there until you reach the 'To Coda' sign, then jump to the coda." Further discussion of the coda sign can be found on page 163.

Example 2-281:

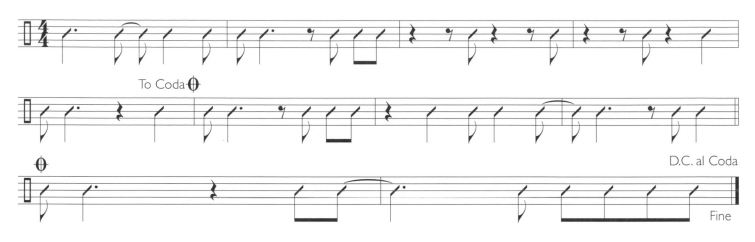

D.C. might also indicate an ending to go to, as in the following example:

Example 2-282:

D.S.

D.S. (Dal Segno) means "from the sign." This is similar to a D.C. except, rather than telling you to return and play from the very beginning of the chart, it tells you to play from wherever you see the "sign." So, unlike D.C., there are two components to a D.S.: the instruction to "D.S." (play from the sign) and the sign itself.

Here is how these are written:

Example 2-283:

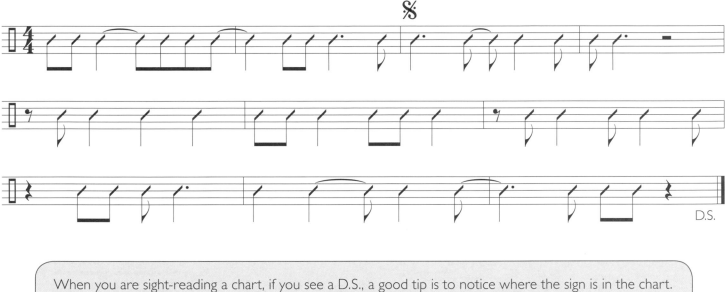

> When you are sight-reading a chart, if you see a D.S., a good tip is to notice where the sign is in the chart. Because it can be anywhere, if you haven't noticed this in advance, you can find yourself reaching the D.S. and your eyes not quickly enough going to the page and measure that has the sign.

Coda Sign

Most commonly used when there is something that happens only at the very end of a song, the coda sign has two components: a "To Coda" and the **Coda** itself ($\oplus$). The former says "jump from here to where you see the Coda sign."

Imagine, for example, that the last four bars of a 32-bar song appears as:

Example 2-284:

At the third bar of the previous example, you would jump to where you saw a coda sign:

Example 2-285:

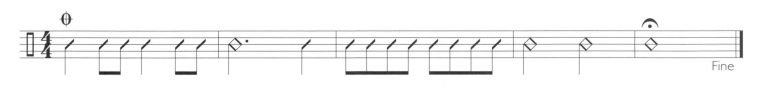

… and continue playing from there until the end ("Fine").

The Coda itself is always indicated by the ⊕, the word "Coda" or both of them together. The indication of the place from which one should jump to the coda may be shown as mentioned above (the words "To Coda"), but it may also be indicated by "To ⊕" or even just a ⊕ (in this case, the reader knows from the context which is the coda itself and which is the indication to jump to it).

Thus, Example 2-281 could also be written in this way:

Example 2-286:

Combining These Elements

These elements (repeats, multiple endings, D.C., D.S., and coda signs) are especially effective at making a chart concise when they are combined. We can combine them in ways such as "D.C. al 2nd ending," "D.S. al Coda," etc.

Notice that we have included **rehearsal letters** A & B in the following example.

Example 2-287:

Let's be sure you are clear about what happens in the above example. We play the "A" section through the 1st ending; then the "A" section through the 2nd ending; then the "B" section; then we "D.C." to the beginning of the "A" section and take it to the 3rd ending. At the end of the 6 bars of the 3rd ending, we "D.S." back to the 2nd bar of the "A" section, and play it for a few bars until we follow the "To Coda" to the Coda sign, and play from there until the end ("Fine").

In this example, we played a total of 46 bars of music, yet there were only 27 bars needed to write it. For example, we played the second bar of "A" a total of four times, yet only had to write it once. As you can see, these road map signs save us from writing the same bars multiple times.

Appendix V – Articulation and Pause Marks

Let's examine articulation and pause marks, which convey information about how the music is to be phrased when it is performed. But first, let's consider the importance of context: how the use and meaning of articulation marks varies by period, style, and instrument.

The Importance of Context

Articulation marks had limited use in early music; look at Bach's music and you will see few: some slurs, and the dynamics *f* (forte) and *p* (piano) (but not *mf*, *ff*, etc.). When musicians share a common language/style, the need for articulation marks is minimal, as the performers understand how the music is to be played. In the world of classical music, there has been an evolution since Bach's time towards the use of more and more articulation marks. Observe the progression from Bach to Mozart to Beethoven to Berlioz to Wagner to Mahler to Schoenberg to Ligeti: each composer gives more and more information to guide the performers (articulation marks, dynamics, notes to performers), as each is writing for performers who share less of a common style and each composer's music becomes a "style" of its own. Meanwhile, performers began to try to get more and more into the minds of the composers and perform the music exactly as the composers intended. This is indicative both of a historical evolution and the disappearance of a common language/style.

In writing jazz and contemporary music, it helps to know who will be reading the music. If the performers share a common language, few articulation marks and notes are necessary; if, however, you are writing for musicians who are not fluent and immersed in the style (e.g. a jazz suite for a group that includes symphony musicians), it is advisable to specify more articulations.

An articulation mark can also mean different things, depending on the style and era of the music and the instrument for which it is written. In *Form and Performance*, Erwin Stein quotes classical pianist Artur Schnabel who, asked by a student whether he should play a passage staccato, replied: "Which staccato do you mean, No. 7 or No. 56?" In fact, there are multiple variations of staccato marks used in classical music but rarely in any other style. Musicians will interpret the same passage differently, depending on era, instrument, and style (for example, by default, jazz brass and woodwind players will slur every eighth note; classical players, reading the same passage, would tongue every eighth note unless there are slur marks).

Robert Sadin, a great source of guidance on this topic, gives an interesting example in Giuseppe Verdi's penultimate opera, *Otello*. In the last act, 16 bars before the cello "Lo stesso movimento" section, the flute, clarinet, and bassoon have several bars of music in which many notes are marked with the hat (also called "rooftop," "vertical accent," "martellato," or, incorrectly but not uncommonly, "marcato") symbol while the strings, playing the same passage along with the woodwinds, have these notes marked with the regular accent symbol. Sadin feels that, when woodwinds playing music of that period see a regular accent, they tongue the notes, playing them more sharply, so Verdi used the hat symbol to get them to "sink into" the notes more, not just to tongue them, and therefore to get the same phrasing that the violins produce when they see accent marks. Thus, Verdi used different articulation symbols for different instruments in order to get the same result.

Just a few bars later in *Otello*, however, Verdi uses the hat symbol for the solo cello, wanting to make sure that the cello gets the full sound out of the note (not an emphasis on attack at the expense of producing the note sound). Sadin points out that, unlike in jazz where the hat symbol indicates a stronger attack than an accent mark, in Verdi it means that the tone of the note is more emphasized.

Another example of composers meaning different things when they use an articulation mark: in Claude Debussy's *Jeux: Poème dansé*, he has a series of four eighth notes, the first with a tenuto mark and the remaining three with staccato marks. In his written instructions to the performer, he writes in French what translates to "make the accent," so he means for the tenuto mark to imply accent, not just that the tone of that note is sustained for longer; a contemporary musician would not assume there is any accent implied by a tenuto mark.

Finally, in modern music (20th and 21st century classical music, etc.), there may even be articulation marks invented by an individual composer to indicate unusual special techniques to be used in a specific piece (these must be explained in notes that the composer includes with the written music).

Therefore, please understand that the following description of articulation marks is just a starting place, and you will need to consider the era and style of music as well as the instrument for which the music is written in order to know the context you need to correctly perform it.

Articulation Marks

In this brief and basic review of articulation marks other than the staccato (which was introduced in *THE RHYTHM BOOK—Beginning Notation and Sight-Reading*), we will not discuss every possible mark: there are many that are rarely used, or pertain only to certain instruments (e.g. details of bowing a stringed instrument, or bending strings on guitar, or slapping an electric bass string). So, this overview of articulation marks will focus only on these commonly used articulation marks: the tenuto, legato, accent, and hat marks, as well as ghost notes and slurs. Then we briefly examine a few pause marks: the fermata, railroad tracks, and breath mark. For each, I have used the name I most frequently hear used for it, but mention alternatives.

Tenuto

The **tenuto** (sometimes called portamento, although the latter can also refer to "sliding" from one note to the next) **mark** (−) is used to indicate that we want a note to be sustained for its full notated value. If it is followed by another note, for example, one should minimize the time between notes in which there is no sound. The tenuto mark is sort of the opposite of the staccato mark. Here is an example of using the tenuto mark:

Example 2-288:

As you can see in the following example, tenuto and staccato marks can be intermixed even within a single phrase:

Example 2-289:

> In classical music, a tenuto mark is sometimes used to mean "hold the note slightly longer than its full value" which is done by introducing a brief slight rubato, and in this way to give the note special emphasis.
> We would not expect this meaning in most other styles of music, particularly any style of music that is grooving (i.e. played in time with a rhythm section). The previousy mentioned use by Debussy, in which tenuto also is meant to imply accent, is another, if less common, possibility.

Slur/Legato

Like the symbol for a tie, the **slur** is a curved line that goes under or over notes, generally on the side of the note heads.

Example 2-290:

Ties should directly connect two note heads; slurs can be placed close to two notes or be placed above or below a series of notes. When there is a curved line between two notes, you can avoid confusing a slur with a tie by remembering that a tie always connects notes of the same pitch, and a slur is applied to notes with different pitches.

Example 2-291:

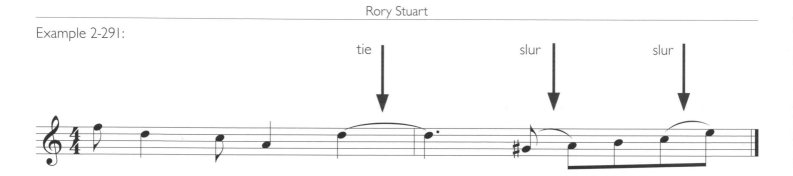

This curved line is a symbol that is a bit more complex than the others we are discussing because it indicates articulation in a way that is different and specific for each instrument (for example, saxophone: slight use of the tongue while sustaining air flow; guitar: pull-offs and hammer-ons without picking; string instruments: played as part of one full bow stroke); and, it can also indicate a phrase (e.g. in piano music).

But, regardless of the instrument-specific technique involved, the musical effect produced is known as **legato**. Like tenuto, legato (which translates from Italian as "bound together") means that notes are sustained for their full value so that there is no silence between adjacent notes, but also that the attack of each note is minimized. Unlike tenuto, there is no implication that a note under a slur sign would get extra duration or emphasis.

> As discussed above, articulation marks must be understood in the context of era, style, and instrument. With regard to instrument-specific interpretation, curved lines are an interesting case. For example, a saxophonist can blow a steady stream of air, but either choose to make a slight tongue-produced "perforation" between notes, which would still be called legato, or not use the tongue at all, which would better be described as slurring. A pianist may create the illusion of legato by sustaining notes for their full value and playing very smoothly and evenly, or may interpret the curved line as indicating phrasing rather than legato. So, even for a particular instrument, there is some interpretation based on musical context, and sometimes even some ambiguity.

Be careful to make a clear visual distinction, as noted above, between the tie—which should connect directly from one note head of the same pitch to another—and the slur, which should be placed under or over two or more notes that are not the same pitch (often a group of notes). While we can use both ties and slurs with rhythmic notation (here, the first five notes are slurred, and the note at the end of the first bar is tied to the first note in the second bar):

Example 2-292:

… the use of pitches makes it more clear that it is a tie rather than a slur between the bars:

Example 2-293:

Accent

The **accent** (also called marcato—but see the sidebar below) **mark** (>) indicates that a note should be played with more emphasis ("accented"). The attack of the note is especially stressed:

Example 2-294:

Here, the use of the accent mark is shown with pitches:

Example 2-295:

Hat

What is informally known as the **hat** (also called martellato, rooftop, strong accent, vertical accent, or incorrectly but not uncommonly marcato) **mark** (ʌ) can have many different meanings depending on context, as discussed above. Generally, it is used to mean that a note gets emphasis and (e.g. in jazz, to indicate an especially strong accent) but that the sound (or "body") of the note is held more, and that the note itself is heavier, rather than the quick attack and decay that may be played when a horn player sees an accent mark; but even this description depends on style and instrument. Like the accent mark, the hat can be also be combined with other marks (staccato or tenuto). Here it is shown with rhythmic notation:

Example 2-296:

… and here with pitches:

Example 2-297:

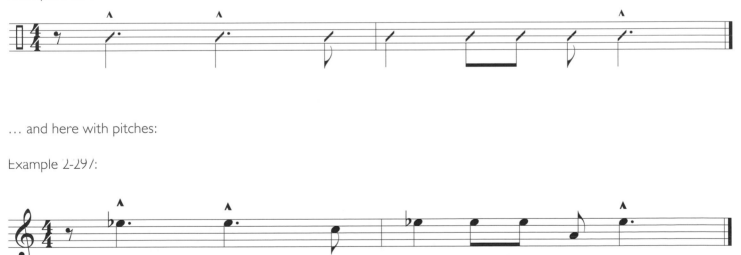

"Marcato" is an example of a term about which there is some confusion. It is "correctly" used to describe the accent, not the hat, and the hat is "correctly" described by the term martellato. However, in common practice there is some confusion, and "marcato" is sometimes used to describe the hat!

Ghost Note

What is the opposite of an accented note? Especially in jazz (though rarely in classical music), we may want to indicate a note that is played with such a lack of emphasis that it may be more "felt" than sounded. This is called a **ghost note**. In "ghosting" a note, we may make it a very unemphasized note whose pitch can still be identified, and this would be indicated:

Example 2-298:

... while, if the pitch itself cannot be heard clearly enough to be identified, but the note is still felt, we can write it this way (sometimes, these "X" note heads might also be put in parentheses):

Example 2-299:

Pause Marks

There are a few standard markings that indicate a pause to the performer. Here is a brief description of the three of these you will see most often: the fermata, railroad tracks, and breath mark.

Fermata

The **fermata** (sometimes informally called a bird's eye) **mark** (⌢) tells us to sustain a pitch (or rest) while time is suspended. Typically we hold it for a while, or even indefinitely until someone cues to end it. It often happens at the end of a piece, but can happen anywhere.

Example 2-300:

Railroad Tracks

The **railroad tracks** (more formally called caesura) (//) tells us to take a brief pause in the music—to momentarily suspend the time before resuming at tempo. Unlike a fermata over a rest (which would be held for indefinite duration until a cue to resume at the tempo of the piece), the caesura is a pause that is always short in duration.

Example 2-301:

Breath Mark

The **breath mark** (also called luftpause) (❜) tells us to take a breath—either literally (for wind instruments, e.g. reeds or brass) or figuratively (for others). We give the sense of momentarily pausing in the phrasing, without suspension of the underlying tempo:

Example 2-302:

Combining Articulation Marks

Articulation marks can be combined in a single phrase and, in some cases, even simultaneously applied to a single note. Here, we combine many articulation marks in a single example (for the sake of demonstration, this has more than we would normally see in a mere four bars; I hope it is more than you ever have to use! Also, we would likely use far fewer articulation marks for performers who are familiar with the style in which the composer writes):

Example 2-303:

> For more information on articulation marks, including some of the less commonly used ones, there are easily found resources on the web. At the time I am writing this, one good reference is at http://www.dolmetsch.com/musictheory21.htm. In classical music, as I mentioned before, there are several marks that indicate different degrees of staccato; unless you perform in the classical genre, these may not be worth studying. For the best description of the articulation marks that are specific to an instrument, especially those used to convey special modern techniques, see instrument-specific books devoted to this topic (for example: *The Other Flute: A Performance Manual of Twentieth Century Techniques* by Robert Dick).

Appendix VI – A Brief Guide to Choices, Rules, and Style in Rhythm Notation

Here is a summary of some of the rhythmic notation choices one faces, and the important rules vs. the personal preference and stylistic choices. I will in particular contrast my personal style ("Rory-style"), that of my colleague, saxophonist Arun Luthra ("Arun-style"), and what I've seen in classical music ("classical-style"):

Analyzing Required Beats

Question: A lot of what is discussed in the book revolves around the required beats to show (which informs how to beam, what beats not to show, etc..), which is in turn based on the level (finest division, i.e. underlying grid) of the music. Should the "level of the music" be determined on the basis of a chart, a section, a bar, or beat by beat?

Answer: Because there can be such dramatic changes within a composition or even within a section, there is insufficient argument for looking on such a large scale to make this determination. But there are two styles that are equally accepted and reasonable: determining the level on a measure-by-measure basis, or on a beat-by-beat basis. My colleague, Arun Luthra, prefers to do this on a beat-by-beat basis, so he would write the following, as long as this were a 4/4 + 3/4 kind of 7/4, and would use a dotted bar line between the fourth and fifth beats (I haven't shown the dotted bar line here, but want you to focus on what happens on the third and fourth beats):

Example 2-304:

… while I generally do this on a measure-by-measure basis and would write (again, notice the third and fourth beats):

Example 2-305:

The classical music world, with pieces that are studied extensively before being played in public, and with its Euro-centric rhythmic concept, is much less consistent with this, and, in some cases, does not show what I would consider to be required beats, also not uncommonly beaming across barlines in order to indicate phrases. This approach wouldn't work as well in a situation with an Afro-centric time concept and parts that must be sight-read without prior study.

So, Rory-style: bar by bar and never beam across beats or barlines; Arun-style: beat by beat and never beam across beats or barlines; classical-style: anything goes.

Note: even with Rory-style, it is fine to have an extended rest at the beginning or end of the bar that does not show every required beat. For example, at 16th-note level in 7/4, where every quarter note should be shown, I see nothing wrong with having a dotted half note rest in the last three beats of the bar.

Beaming Notes

In discussing rules and choices for beaming notes, let's first note the "vocal chart caveat": if you are writing a vocal chart with the old style conventions, no note is beamed to any other note (except, in some cases, if different notes are sung while holding the same syllable). There are obvious disadvantages with this, especially for a vocalist who is sight-reading more modern syncopated music; most vocal charts written in this old style did not have much syncopation and rhythmic complexity (and the music was often limited to the eighth-note level), so these disadvantages were not such an issue. Many current high-level vocalists I know would prefer charts be written for them with beaming as would be done for any instrumentalist. The remainder of our discussion assumes you are not engaged in this old style of vocal part writing.

Question: In 4/4 music at the eighth-note level, should you beam by quarter or by half note? Here we beam by half note:

Example 2-306:

… and here by quarter note:

Example 2-307:

Answer: To follow the logic of showing and grouping by required beat, it is clear that we should beam by half note. Arun-style: always beam this by half note, as shown in Example 2-306; classical-style: usually but not always beam by half note; Rory-style: either is acceptable and easy to read.

Question: In deciding how to beam and what beats to show, which takes priority, the beat we feel in the meter, or our rule about how required beats to show are determined by note rate? In this example, the pulse felt in 13/8 is the eighth note, and the 13/8 is felt as four short, a long, and a short pulse (SSSSLS). If we write this to show each eighth note, and beam by eighth note, we would write it this way:

Example 2-308:

If we write it beaming by quarter note (except by dotted quarter on the "long pulse"), because that is what our rule for 16th-note level tells us to do, we would write it like this:

Example 2-309:

Answer: Classical-style would typically write it the first way (and this is the default for notation programs such as Finale); Rory-style and Arun-style both give priority to how the meter is felt and, for SSSSLS, say that the second way is much easier to read and always preferable.

Question: We want to beam triple meter 16th note music by the dotted quarter note, and we want to avoid ties within the beat. But, in some cases, it is not possible to do both. Which is better, this way:

Example 2-310:

… or one of these ways?

Example 2-311:

Answer: None of these choices seem great. According to "Rory-style," Example 2-310 has the problem that it's difficult for one's eye to see where each dotted quarter (i.e. each beat in 12/8) begins. "Arun-style" gives some preference to showing the third eighth of each dotted quarter, so tends to prefer the first line of Example 2-311, and would beam it slightly differently (see the next to last beat):

Example 2-312:

Rory-style notes there could be other considerations, e.g. if the other parts being played in the piece cause one to feel a certain way of dividing the dotted-quarter beat. But assuming that does not come into play, Rory-style prefers some hybrid that might look like this (and Arun-style also likes this):

Example 2-313:

This version preserves the ease with which the reader's eye can pinpoint the beginning of each dotted quarter, but simplifies Example 2-312.

Question: When should you break secondary beams, and when should you leave them unbroken?

Answer: The beam furthest from the note heads is called the primary beam; all the other beams are called secondary beams. Although it doesn't affect the rhythmic values of the notes, we can choose to break secondary beams when this helps with readability. In general, when we write music faster than 16th notes, we should break secondary beams to show "required beats." For example, at the 32nd-note level, we should show each eighth note. The best way to do this is to beam the entire quarter note together (for example if we are in 4/4), yet break the secondary beams to show each eighth note and tie across eighth notes if necessary.

Of course we do not want to write this way, where we fail to show required beats (each eighth note):

Example 2-314:

… but this way, while not "wrong," makes it unnecessarily difficult to read by not breaking the secondary beams:

Example 2-315:

… and this way, while (arguably—see above) acceptable in 8/8, is not good in 4/4 since we should be feeling each quarter note and should therefore beam each quarter by primary beam:

Example 2-316:

This way, beaming each quarter note, but breaking the secondary beams at each eighth note, is best:

Example 2-317:

At times, classical-style might use the notations shown in Example 2-315 and Example 2-316, but Rory-style says Example 2-317 is far preferable, and Arun-style says that is the correct way, as well.

Beaming Rests

There are a number of choices to make regarding rests and whether to beam them. For example, at the 16th-note level, we can beam all the rests in a required beat:

Example 2-318:

… or only the rests that are in between notes:

Example 2-319:

…or not beam any rests:

Example 2-320:

The same choices apply at other levels. Here, at the eighth level, beaming all rests in the half note:

Example 2-321:

… or only the rests that are in between notes:

Example 2-322:

… or not beam any rests:

Example 2-323:

Question: Should you beam rests at the eighth level? If so, how?

Answer: Classical-style: I've seen all these variations used; Arun-style: do not beam rests at all the eighth level; also, the note on the last beat should be a quarter note with a staccato mark, because no rests on "ands" at eighth note level; Rory-style: all of these are okay, except for my concern with beaming together three eighth notes, or any group of three notes in a duple meter, described below.

If we do beam rests, we have a choice whether to half-stem the rests:

Example 2-324:

… or not:

Example 2-325:

Question: Should you beam rests at the 16th level and beyond? If so, how? Should you use half stems for the rests or not?

Answer: Classical-style: anything goes regarding beaming; classical music has generally not used half stems for rests. For example, Hindemith does not use half stems, and he beams rests that are between 16th notes in a beat, but not rests that are part of the beat before or after the written notes; Rory-style: I strongly prefer beaming rests for the entire beat, especially in cases where contiguous rests in adjacent beats might confuse the eye as to beat boundary; I have no preference between half-stemmed rests or rests without half-stems. Arun-style: always beam the rests except at eighth level, and always use half-stems when you beam a rest. The half-stem of the rest must match the rhythmic value of the rest. Thus, Arun-style says that Example 2-324 would be the only way this should be written except that, since Arun-style determines required beats on a beat-by-beat rather than bar-by-bar basis, and says that at the eighth level there should never be a rest on the "and", that example should actually be written:

Example 2-326:

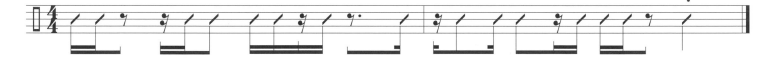

Question: What is the issue with beaming together groups of three notes in a duple meter? Is it alright to do this?

Answer: Sometimes, people write triplets without using a triplet sign, and assume that the reader will understand they are triplets because they are beamed together and because of the number of beats in the bar. I do not recommend doing this, not ever! I always use a triplet sign if I write a triplet. But, because some people omit the triplet sign, if we see a chart in 4/4, for example, and it has three notes beamed together, there is at least a moment in which the reader has to evaluate whether this is a triplet without a triplet sign:

Example 2-327:

To avoid this distraction, I generally do not beam together groups of three notes in a duple meter; I would either beam to include the rests:

Example 2-328:

… or, at the eighth note level, beam fewer notes to avoid this:

Example 2-329:

Because Arun-style never beams rests at the eighth note level and never beams groups of three eighth notes in 4/4, only this last example would be correct.

Note Durations, Rests, and Staccato

Question: Are there certain places where we should avoid placing a rest? Which of these is preferable, and are all acceptable?

Example 2-330:

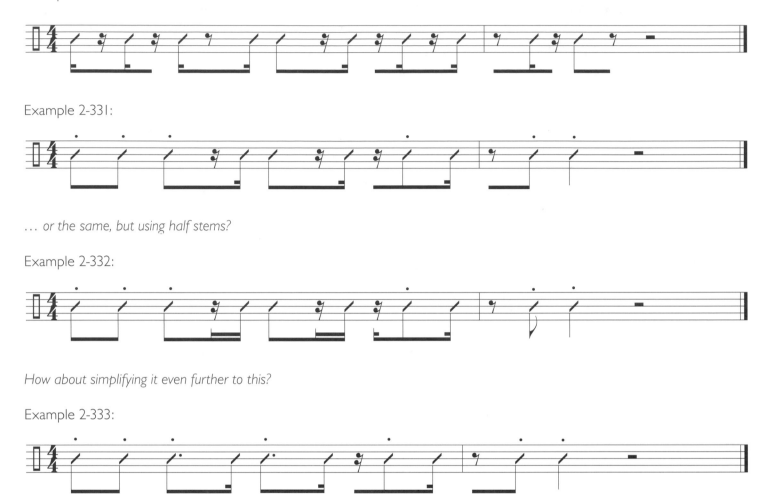

Example 2-331:

... or the same, but using half stems?

Example 2-332:

How about simplifying it even further to this?

Example 2-333:

Answer: Classical music: Example 2-330 is very common, as would be the same thing without beaming the rests. Arun-style: Example 2-332 is the correct way, and the only correct way, to write this music. Arun-style says never place rests on the "and" in eighth note-level music, or on the "e" and "a" in 16th note-level music, and always half-stem 16th note rests. Example 2-333 is not to be used because Arun-style says it is against the rules to put a staccato mark on a dotted note (he feels it is a contradiction to both tell readers to sustain the note longer by dotting it, and also tell them to make it short by putting a staccato mark on it). Rory-style: There are cases of using voices or sustaining instruments such as strings or horns, especially at very slow tempos, where precise cut-offs of notes might justify some special use of rests. Otherwise, make it as simple to read as possible while still sounding as the writer intends. Example 2-331 or Example 2-332 or Example 2-333 are all good, their intention is clear. It's true that, in common practice, one does not see staccato marks on whole notes or half notes much. But, since I'm fine with a staccato mark being place on a quarter note, why not with one being placed on a note that is three-fourths as long (i.e. a dotted eighth)? It's not common practice, but I don't mind it.

Question: If writing for an instrument with limited sustain (e.g. a banjo, marimba, cowbell, woodblock), can we show notes the long way (if it makes for easier-to-read notation) or must we write the notes the short way? For example, is this acceptable:

Example 2-334:

... or must it be written this way?:

Example 2-335:

Answer: Classical-style: this would very likely be written showing the note values as short. Rory-style: especially if this is an instrument such as marimba or banjo playing this line along with instruments who were sustaining it as in Example 2-334, I wouldn't hesitate to write it the same way it is shown in that example, especially if it were easier to read that way. Arun-style says that notation with sustained notes is almost always more difficult to read than short-note notation so, in this case Example 2-335 is preferable; there is almost never a reason to write sustained notes except for an instrument that can sustain them.

Question: Are there any differences in what should be written with rests versus what should be written with notes?

Answer: Yes, by convention, even though some of these conventions may not seem entirely logical. In 4/4, we would write the first note as a dotted quarter:

Example 2-336:

... but, by convention, professional music copyists would not write the first rest as a dotted quarter rest, they would write a separate quarter rest and eighth rest:

Example 2-337:

Professional-copyist-style and Arun-style: do not dot a quarter rest in 4/4. Classical-style and Rory-style: it's fine either way.

By contrast, in a triple meter, if we replace the first dotted quarter note:

Example 2-338:

... by a rest, it too should be a dotted quarter rest, and all styles agree on this:

Example 2-339:

What about other kinds of rests in 4/4? Classical-style and Rory-style both say this is okay:

Example 2-340:

... but Arun-style says it should be this:

Example 2-341:

Classical-style and Rory-style say the last beat of this example is fine:

Example 2-342:

... but Arun-style dictates that, because there should not be any rests on "e" or "a" at the 16th level, it should be written with a last beat shown this way:

Example 2-343:

(Rory-style likes the last note being a staccato quarter, but allows for the other version in music where the duration of the note needs to be indicated precisely. Usually, it does not!)

In classical music, one often finds the figure shown on the first beat written this way:

Example 2-344:

... but, in Arun-style, it should be written this way:

Example 2-345:

... and in Rory-style, the Arun-style way would be great, but even this would be acceptable:

Example 2-346:

Pickups

Question: Can you have a pickup (also called "anacrusis" in classical music) longer than one bar? Longer than two bars? What's the longest pickup you can have?

Answer: In principle there is no reason a pickup should not be able to last longer than one bar, but, in practice, it is rare to see. Certainly, if we count off 4/4 this way:

Example 2-347:

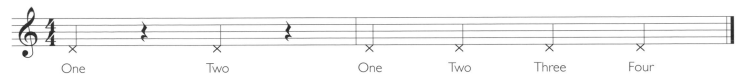

… anything after the third beat of the first bar of the countoff is a practical possibility:

Example 2-348:

Of course, we would not normally notate the countoff, so that example would be written:

Example 2-349:

(Unfortunately, it's still not clear in that notation whether only the first bar or the first two bars would be a pickup with respect to the beginning of the music.)

Question: In a pickup, should there ever be rests before the first written note? If so, what is the rule about what rests to show?

Answer: You never want to fill in all the rests in the bar with a pickup, or there will be no way for the reader to know it is a pickup. So, if this example began with a pickup, we would never write it like this:

Example 2-350:

... but always like this:

Example 2-351:

... and, instead of this:

Example 2-352:

... always this:

Example 2-353:

Because by far the most common problem students have is to write rests before a pickup where they should not be, I start by giving them the rule of thumb to "never put rests before a pickup." However, there are cases where, especially if the music is at the 16th level or below, filling out the first beat in which notes happen can make for easier reading. Instead of this:

Example 2-354:

... I would actually prefer this:

Example 2-355:

... and, instead of this:

Example 2-356:

... I would definitely prefer either this:

Example 2-357:

... or this:

Example 2-358:

(I bracket the triplet in the pickup for visual clarity, Arun-style would not.)

Arun-style puts this into the form of a rule: at faster than eighth-note level, begin notation of a pickup on a beat, even if that requires rests before the notes of the pickup.

Miscellaneous

Question: Is it ever advisable to use double dotted or triple dotted notes? Or double dotted or triple dotted rests?

Answer: Classical-style, we often see double dotted notes, e.g.:

Example 2-359:

... but Rory-style says one must show required beats. If you do that, you will rarely ever use a double dotted note. The above example would better be written:

Example 2-360:

Arun-style makes some exceptions about showing required beats, and, for example, in 4/4 allows a double dotted half note on the first beat followed by an eighth note, or a double dotted quarter note on the first or third beat followed by a flagged 16th note.

Note: for further questions about how to notate in odd meters, and how to choose which way to write an odd meter, see *THE RHYTHM BOOK—Odd Meters and Changing Meters*. For different ways of showing metric modulations and rhythmic superimpositions, as well as when to use subdivision, see *THE RHYTHM BOOK—Superimposition and Subdivision, Metric Modulation, Feel Modulation and Displacement*.

About the Author

New York-based jazz guitarist and composer Rory Stuart has led critically acclaimed groups and played as a sideman with a number of major figures in the history of jazz. Described as "perhaps THE most innovative straight-ahead jazz guitarist to emerge in years," by *Jazz Times*, Rory has led the rhythm curriculum since 1992 at the world-renowned New School for Jazz and Contemporary Music. A list of his former students reads like a "Who's Who" of rising young jazz stars.

The recipient of awards from the National Endowment for the Arts, Meet the Composer, and the Fulbright Commission, he has directed jazz workshops in Italy, Singapore, and Korea, and performed and taught around the world, including in Argentina, Austria, the Bahamas, Brazil, Canada, Chile, Columbia, the Czech Republic, Denmark, Germany, Greece, Israel, Iceland, India, Israel, Italy, Kazakhstan, Korea, Poland, Portugal, Spain, Sweden, Switzerland, and the USA.

For more information, please see www.rorystuart.com.

About the Rhythm Book series:

THE RHYTHM BOOK—Beginning Notation and Sight-Reading:
• introduces rhythmic notation, from the very first steps (does not assume you have any notation background);
• teaches how to read and write rhythms in 4/4 at the quarter, eighth, and triplet eighth levels;
• creates a solid foundation on which further notation and sight-reading skills can be built.

THE RHYTHM BOOK—Intermediate Notation and Sight-Reading:
• builds from knowledge of quarter, eighth, and triplet eighths;
• progresses systematically from 16th notes through triplets of all rates, triple meters, odd meters, and even 32nd notes and beyond;
• prepares you to read and correctly write nearly any rhythm you will ordinarily encounter.

THE RHYTHM BOOK—Rhythmic Development and Performance in 4/4: Master rhythmic performance in 4/4. This volume:
• examines rhythmic styles and feels, including swing, Afro-Cuban, Brazilian, funk, calypso, reggae, and ballads;
• discusses phrasing, relationship to the beat, feeling time and form, defining the time in your playing, very fast and slow tempos, playing with others and rhythmically interacting, and how to develop rhythm ideas;
• includes numerous examples, as well as worksheets for suggested transcription projects.

THE RHYTHM BOOK—Crossrhythms on 4/4: Crossrhythms (a.k.a. implicit polymeter or groupings) are a powerful tool to expand your vocabulary in performance and composing. Perhaps the most under-represented rhythmic area in musical education, their study brings surprising benefits, including greater depth and freedom over harmonic forms. This volume:
• provides a systematic method for learning any crossrhythm;
• presents crossrhythms on 4/4 comprehensively, from most common/simple to rare/complex;
• incorporates many exercises, and examples from different musical genres.

THE RHYTHM BOOK—Odd Meters and Changing Meters: Aimed at developing the reader's performance and composition skills with odd and changing meters, this volume:
• provides a systematic way to learn any new meter;
• explores odd meters in depth, different flavors of changing meters, and crossrhythms on odd meters;
• includes interesting examples from a wide variety of musical styles, and exercises to develop your mastery.

THE RHYTHM BOOK—Superimposition and Subdivision, Metric Modulation, Feel Modulation and Displacement: With focus on some of the most challenging rhythmic areas in 21st Century music, this volume:
• offers systematic ways to learn rhythm superimpositions and convert between superimposition and subdivision;
• teaches a series of methods for performing metric modulations;
• presents exercises to address the challenges of feel modulation and feel displacement;
• demonstrates how to combine techniques (e.g. crossrhythms at superimposition rates over odd meters).

THE ULTIMATE COLLECTION OF
FAKE BOOKS

The Real Book – Sixth Edition

Hal Leonard proudly presents the first legitimate and legal editions of these books ever produced. These bestselling titles are mandatory for anyone who plays jazz! Over 400 songs, including: All By Myself • Dream a Little Dream of Me • God Bless the Child • Like Someone in Love • When I Fall in Love • and more.

00240221 Volume 1, C Edition $39.99
00240224 Volume 1, B♭ Edition $39.99
00240225 Volume 1, E♭ Edition $39.99
00240226 Volume 1, BC Edition $39.99
00240222 Volume 2, C Edition $39.99
00240227 Volume 2, B♭ Edition $39.99
00240228 Volume 2, E♭ Edition $39.99

Best Fake Book Ever – 4th Edition

More than 1,000 songs from all styles of music, including: All My Loving • At the Hop • Cabaret • Dust in the Wind • Fever • From a Distance • Hello, Dolly! • Hey Jude • King of the Road • Longer • Misty • Route 66 • Sentimental Journey • Somebody • Song Sung Blue • Spinning Wheel • Unchained Melody • We Will Rock You • What a Wonderful World • Wooly Bully • Y.M.C.A. • and more.

00290239 C Edition $49.99
00240083 B♭ Edition $49.95
00240084 E♭ Edition $49.95

Classic Rock Fake Book – 2nd Edition

This fake book is a great compilation of more than 250 terrific songs of the rock era, arranged for piano, voice, guitar and all C instruments. Includes: All Right Now • American Woman • Birthday • Honesty • I Shot the Sheriff • I Want You to Want Me • Imagine • It's Still Rock and Roll to Me • Lay Down Sally • Layla • My Generation • Rock and Roll All Nite • Spinning Wheel • White Room • We Will Rock You • lots more!

00240108 ....$35.00

Classical Fake Book – 2nd Edition

This unprecedented, amazingly comprehensive reference includes over 850 classical themes and melodies for all classical music lovers. Includes everything from Renaissance music to Vivaldi and Mozart to Mendelssohn. Lyrics in the original language are included when appropriate.

00240044 ....$39.99

The Disney Fake Book – 4th Edition

Even more Disney favorites, including: The Bare Necessities • Can You Feel the Love Tonight • Circle of Life • How Do You Know? • Let It Go • Part of Your World • Reflection • Some Day My Prince Will Come • When I See an Elephant Fly • You'll Be in My Heart • and many more.

00175311 Melody/Lyrics/Chords $30.00

The Folksong Fake Book

Over 1,000 folksongs perfect for performers, school teachers, and hobbyists. Includes: Bury Me Not on the Lone Prairie • Clementine • Danny Boy • The Erie Canal • Go, Tell It on the Mountain • Home on the Range • Kumbaya • Michael Row the Boat Ashore • Shenandoah • Simple Gifts • Swing Low, Sweet Chariot • When Johnny Comes Marching Home • Yankee Doodle • and many more.

00240151 ....$24.95

The Hymn Fake Book

Nearly 1,000 multi-denominational hymns perfect for church musicians or hobbyists: Amazing Grace • Christ the Lord Is Risen Today • For the Beauty of the Earth • It Is Well with My Soul • A Mighty Fortress Is Our God • O for a Thousand Tongues to Sing • Praise to the Lord, the Almighty • Take My Life and Let It Be • What a Friend We Have in Jesus • and hundreds more!

00240145 ....$24.95

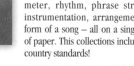

The Nashville Number System Fake Book

The Nashville Number System is the standard way for a professional country musician to notate a song. In essence, a Nashville number chart conveys the harmony, key, meter, rhythm, phrase structure, instrumentation, arrangement, and form of a song – all on a single piece of paper. This collections includes 200 country standards!

00143189 ....$19.99

The Praise & Worship Fake Book – 2nd Edition

Over 400 songs including: Amazing Grace (My Chains Are Gone) • Cornerstone • Everlasting God • Great Are You Lord • In Christ Alone • Mighty to Save • Open the Eyes of My Heart • Shine, Jesus, Shine • This Is Amazing Grace • Your Grace Is Enough • and more.

00160838 C Instruments $34.99

The R&B Fake Book – 2nd Edition

This terrific fake book features 375 classic R&B hits: Baby Love • Best of My Love • Dancing in the Street • Easy • Get Ready • Heatwave • Here and Now • Just Once • Let's Get It On • The Loco-Motion • (You Make Me Feel Like) A Natural Woman • One Sweet Day • Papa Was a Rollin' Stone • Save the Best for Last • September • Sexual Healing • Shop Around • Still • Tell It Like It Is • Up on the Roof • Walk on By • What's Going On • more!

00240107 C Edition $29.95

The Ultimate Christmas Fake Book – 6th Edition

The 6th edition of this bestseller features over 270 traditional and contemporary Christmas hits: Have Yourself a Merry Little Christmas • I'll Be Home for Christmas O Come, All Ye Faithful (Adeste Fideles) • Santa Baby • Winter Wonderland • and more.

00147215 ....$27.50

The Ultimate Country Fake Book – 5th Edition

This book includes over 700 of your favorite country hits: Always on My Mind • Boot Scootin' Boogie • Crazy • Down at the Twist and Shout • Forever and Ever, Amen • Friends in Low Places • The Gambler • Jambalaya • King of the Road • Sixteen Tons • There's a Tear in My Beer • Your Cheatin' Heart • and hundreds more.

00240049 ....$49.99

The Ultimate Fake Book – 5th Edition

Includes over 1,200 hits: Blue Skies • Body and Soul • Endless Love • Isn't It Romantic? • Memory • Mona Lisa • Moon River • Operator • Piano Man • Roxanne • Satin Doll • Shout • Small World • Smile • Speak Softly, Love • Strawberry Fields Forever • Tears in Heaven • Unforgettable • hundreds more!

00240024 C Edition $49.99
00240026 B♭ Edition $49.95
00240025 E♭ Edition $49.95

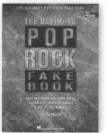

The Ultimate Pop/ Rock Fake Book – 4th Edition

Over 600 pop standards and contemporary hits, including: All Shook Up • Another One Bites the Dust • Crying • Don't Know Much • Dust in the Wind • Earth Angel • Every Breath You Take • Hero • Hey Jude • Hold My Hand • Imagine • Layla • The Loco-Motion • Oh, Pretty Woman • On Broadway • Spinning Wheel • Stand by Me • Stayin' Alive • Tears in Heaven • True Colors • The Twist • Vision of Love • A Whole New World • Wild Thing • Wooly Bully • Yesterday • more!

00240099 ....$39.99

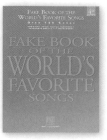

Fake Book of the World's Favorite Songs – 4th Edition

Over 700 favorites, including: America the Beautiful • Anchors Aweigh • Battle Hymn of the Republic • Bill Bailey, Won't You Please Come Home • Chopsticks • Für Elise • His Eye Is on the Sparrow • I Wonder Who's Kissing Her Now • Jesu, Joy of Man's Desiring • My Old Kentucky Home • Sidewalks of New York • Take Me Out to the Ball Game • When the Saints Go Marching In • and hundreds more!

00240072 ....$24.99

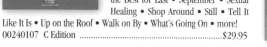
HAL•LEONARD®

Complete songlists available online at
www.halleonard.com

0318